DI006843

MORE PRAISE FOR

Focus on the Good Stuff

"Mike Robbins brilliantly teaches us how to bring more appreciation and gratitude into our lives, our relationships, and our world. His new voice and fresh perspective are powerful. I highly recommend this book."

Marianne Williamson, author, *A Return to Love*

"Mike Robbins' work calls forth the angels of our better nature. I have worked with many in the last year of their life, and it is precisely these remarkable qualities of appreciation and gratitude that leave people and their loved ones with a sense of kindness and clarity of heart. Mike has offered us a great gift."

Stephen Levine, author, *A Year to Live:*
How to Live This Year as If It Were Your Last

"Mike Robbins understands how the universe truly works. *Focus on the Good Stuff* is a brilliant book that will inspire and uplift you. You will discover how to bring more gratitude into your life with ease and grace."

Lynne Twist, author, *The Soul of Money* and cofounder of the Pachamama Alliance

"Mike Robbins has an amazing ability to inspire people through his passionate, authentic, and open-hearted approach to appreciation. This book will have a positive impact on your life."

Rich Fettke, author, *Extreme Success*

"Mike Robbins reminds us to focus on the very best aspects of ourselves and those around us. Written in his compelling and compassionate voice, this book is much-needed consciousness raising for people who want successful relationships and fulfilling lives."

Susan Page, author, *Why Talking Is Not Enough*

"Mike Robbins is a role model of love and gratitude. His message of appreciation comes from his heart, and there is no one better to teach these important lessons!"

Rich Dutra-St. John, cofounder of Challenge Day and coauthor, *Be the Hero You've Been Waiting For*

"*Focus on the Good Stuff* is a remarkable book. Appreciation, as Mike Robbins teaches, can transform your life and help you attract what you truly want."

Christopher Andersonn, author, *Will You Still Love Me If I Don't Win?*

"Mike Robbins' message of appreciation is powerful. He writes and speaks directly from his heart in a way that makes a real difference. This is a truly transformational book that will change lives."

Lee Glickstein, author, *Be Heard Now!* and founder of Speaking Circles International

"*Focus on the Good Stuff* reveals the secret of bringing more gratitude into your life without resorting to simpering sentiment, sappy prose, or dithering diatribe. Mike Robbins brings a fresh and uplifting approach to the age-old task of learning to love life."

Lisa Earle McLeod, syndicated columnist and coauthor, *Forget Perfect*

focus
on the
good stuff

JB JOSSEY-BASS

focus on the good stuff

The Power of Appreciation

Mike Robbins

Foreword by Richard Carlson

BICENTENNIAL

1807

WILEY

2007

BICENTENNIAL

John Wiley & Sons

Copyright © 2007 by John Wiley & Sons, Inc. All rights reserved.

Published by Jossey-Bass
A Wiley Imprint
989 Market Street, San Francisco, CA 94103-1741   www.josseybass.com

Wiley Bicentennial logo: Richard J. Pacifico

No part of this publication may be reproduced, stored in a retrieval system, or
transmitted in any form or by any means, electronic, mechanical, photocopying,
recording, scanning, or otherwise, except as permitted under Section 107 or 108 of
the 1976 United States Copyright Act, without either the prior written permission
of the publisher, or authorization through payment of the appropriate per-copy fee
to the Copyright Clearance Center, Inc., 222 Rosewood Drive, Danvers, MA 01923,
978-750-8400, fax 978-646-8600, or on the Web at www.copyright.com. Requests
to the publisher for permission should be addressed to the Permissions Department,
John Wiley & Sons, Inc., 111 River Street, Hoboken, NJ 07030, 201-748-6011,
fax 201-748-6008, or online at www.wiley.com/go/permissions.

Limit of Liability/Disclaimer of Warranty: While the publisher and author have used
their best efforts in preparing this book, they make no representations or warranties
with respect to the accuracy or completeness of the contents of this book and specifically disclaim any implied warranties of merchantability or fitness for a particular
purpose. No warranty may be created or extended by sales representatives or written
sales materials. The advice and strategies contained herein may not be suitable for your
situation. You should consult with a professional where appropriate. Neither the publisher nor author shall be liable for any loss of profit or any other commercial damages, including but not limited to special, incidental, consequential, or other damages.

Jossey-Bass books and products are available through most bookstores.
To contact Jossey-Bass directly call our Customer Care Department within the U.S.
at 800-956-7739, outside the U.S. at 317-572-3986, or fax 317-572-4002.

Jossey-Bass also publishes its books in a variety of electronic formats. Some content
that appears in print may not be available in electronic books.

Quote in Chapter Seven from *A Return to Love* by Marianne Williamson. Copyright
© 1992 by Marianne Williamson. Reprinted by permission of HarperCollins
Publishers. Portions reprinted from *A Course in Miracles*. Copyright © 1975 by
Foundation for Inner Peace, Inc. All chapter openings are from *A Course in Miracles*.

Library of Congress Cataloging-in-Publication Data
Robbins, Mike, date.
  Focus on the good stuff : the power of appreciation / Mike Robbins ; foreword
by Richard Carlson.
      p. cm.
  Includes bibliographical references.
  ISBN 978-0-7879-8879-1 (cloth)
  1. Gratitude I. Title.
  BF575.G68R63   2007
  158—dc22   2007007874

Printed in the United States of America
FIRST EDITION
HB Printing   10 9 8 7 6 5 4 3 2

contents

foreword

Appreciation is one of the most important keys to a happy and successful life. And for me, the most important ingredient in writing a book on appreciation is very simple: Does the author walk the talk?

I have had the pleasure of knowing Mike Robbins for a number of years, and I can say, without a shadow of a doubt, that Mike passes the test. He is one of the most genuinely appreciative people I've ever known. He seems to appreciate everyone, everything, and even the gift of life itself—it's almost as though he is on the lookout for something to appreciate. On top of all that, Mike is the most skilled person I've ever known at sharing his appreciation with others in a way that is both authentic and inspiring. It's actually quite amazing to spend some time with him. The most interesting part of Mike's appreciation toward other people as well as life itself is that it's so genuine, and it always comes from his heart. It's never canned or rehearsed, and it's always expressed with sincerity.

Mike Robbins has been teaching the power of appreciation for a number of years to enthusiastic audiences from all walks of life. Companies have him speak to them again and again—almost as though they cannot get enough of such wisdom and common sense.

Being appreciative, expressing appreciation, and receiving appreciation have got to be among the most obvious skills one would seek to learn. Why? Because everyone loves to feel appreciated—it brings out the best in people and makes them act nicer, perform better, and feel better about themselves. When people feel appreciated, they are on top of their game; they are creative, resilient, loyal, and generally fun to be around. In my forty-five years of living, I've yet to hear a single person say to me, "I feel too appreciated." In contrast, I've heard "I don't feel appreciated" thousands of times. So although the value of appreciation seems obvious, it's somewhat rare that someone is well versed in the special and important dynamics of appreciation.

That's why Mike's book is so incredible. He presents here three powerful lessons that you'll be able to put into practice immediately.

1. First, you'll learn about our obsession with "what's wrong" and how that plays out in many of our lives.
2. Next, you'll learn what Mike calls the five principles of appreciation. I read each of them three times before writing this Foreword, and I felt far more equipped to be appreciative than at any other time in my life. In a word, I was stunned at the depth of the material and its immediate impact on my life—and on the lives around me. I found that as I practiced, my two teenagers "magically" were more interested in me again. Was it magic?

Or was it that they felt more appreciated? I think you
know the answer to that question.

3. Finally, you'll learn how to put appreciation into action.
When I am appreciative of the people with whom I
work, I experience happy people who love to be loyal,
ethical, and friendly.

There are forces in our world that encourage us to be
on guard and negative and that fill our minds with self-
doubt. There are millions of people who reinforce this way
of looking at and relating to the world. This book is an anti-
dote to those pressures. Almost immediately upon reading
it, you'll feel a spark in your spirit, a nourishing of your
soul. You'll find yourself saying, "Yes, that's the way I want
to live my life."

Mike Robbins deserves a big congratulations on a job
well done. With so much cynicism and negativity in our
world, it's refreshing when someone like Mike comes along
and reminds us of what's truly important and shows us in
simple language how to use to our advantage one of the
most important ingredients in all of life. Once we learn
what Mike has to teach, we will have the capacity to touch,
in a very positive way, the lives of virtually everyone with
whom we come in contact. Sometimes it will be subtle and
other times it will be dramatic, but genuine appreciation is
a powerful force, one that is also extremely contagious.
When you become a more appreciative person and can also
accept appreciation gracefully when it comes your way, others around you—your coworkers, spouse, lover, children,

parents, friends, even strangers—won't be able to help themselves, as they too will become more appreciative.

It is my great honor to recommend this book with
heartfelt enthusiasm. To me, it should be required reading
for everyone. After all, whom do you know among us who
is too appreciative? Not many, to be sure.

You have taken the first step in becoming a more appreciative and thus happier and more content person. Now
read on and find out exactly how it works. Your life will
transform before your eyes!

November 2006   *Richard Carlson*
                                       Walnut Creek, California

Note: Richard Carlson wrote this Foreword three weeks before
he suddenly and unexpectedly passed away on December 13,
2006. With his death, the world lost a great author, teacher,
and man. I lost a dear friend and a wonderful mentor. I'm
grateful for Richard's friendship, support, and belief in me and
my work.—*Mike Robbins*

For my beautiful and brilliant wife, Michelle,
who gives me so much to be grateful for.
Thank you for bringing such love and appreciation
into my life and into our home.

acknowledgments

I'm filled with gratitude, love, and appreciation as I think of the many people who've contributed not only to the creation of this book but also to my personal growth and development.

First and foremost, Michelle Benoit Robbins, thank you for being my wife, partner, lover, best friend, teacher, and inspiration. I thank God every day that I get to spend my life with you. Thank you for believing in me, for loving me, and for calling me forth to be the very best man, husband, and father I can be. I love you with all of my being.

Samantha Benoit Robbins, thank you for coming into this world and accepting us as your parents. I feel so fortunate to be your daddy. You remind me every day about what truly matters, and I'm grateful for that. Thanks for the magic that you brought with you into this world that helped make this book become a reality, and thanks for bringing so much joy to so many people.

Richard Carlson, my dear friend, mentor, and brother. I miss you so much and still cannot believe you are no longer here with us in physical form. Your soul, your love, and your vision live on through your amazing spirit and through all of us whom you touched so deeply. Thank you for your incredible friendship, your belief in me, and for all that you gave to me. I would not have been able to write this book without your guidance and I would not be who I am today without your incredible influence. Rich Fettke, you've been with me every step of the way in this process, and your generosity has been remarkable. I can't thank you enough for everything you've contributed to me, my life, and this book.

Linda Chester, thank you for your great work on my behalf. I'm honored to have you as an agent and a friend. Alan Rinzler, thanks for pushing me. Your editing made me a much better writer.

Mom (Lois Robbins), thanks for your unwavering loyalty, love, and support of me from day one. I'm grateful that you've always encouraged me to go for it and to reach for my dreams. Dad (Ed Robbins), I miss you and wish you were still here with us in body, though I do feel your presence all the time. Thank you for the great genes and for teaching me that real men can be sensitive and express their true feelings.

Lori Robbins, thanks for teaching me so much about life and for always loving me through thick and thin. I'm grateful to have you as a big sister. Rachel Cohen, thanks for your love, enthusiasm, and for always seeing me clearly. I love being your brother and your friend. Uncle Steve Farrell, you are one of the most powerful, loving, and supportive presences in my life. Thanks for encouraging me to "step out" and to play big in life.

Fred Luskin, I'm grateful to have you in my life, and I so appreciate your honesty and support. Your feedback was invaluable throughout this process, and I'm grateful for your willingness to help me. Frank Marquardt, you were with me at the beginning of this book journey, and you helped me birth this vision. Thank you for your support, coaching, and guidance. Joel Pulliam, thank you for helping me take this project to the level it needed to be to get it out to the world.

Susan Page, thank you for your many inspiring books and for your generous encouragement. You gave me the clarity and focus that I needed to get my book started. Marianne Williamson, thank you for your extraordinary work and for the way you've personally inspired and supported me. You've taught me to be a conscious citizen, and I'm grateful for your wisdom. Susan Ariel Rainbow Kennedy, your work and your message have had a great impact on my life. Thank you for your friendship and for supporting me to make this book dream a reality.

Rich and Yvonne Dutra-St. John, I'm so grateful for the gifts you've given me. Thank you for being such an excellent example of love, commitment, and passion—through your relationship, your work, and the way you each live your lives. Chris Andersonn, you have no idea what a miracle you've been in my life these past thirteen years. Meeting you was the turning point in my spiritual evolution. Thank you for teaching me to connect with myself, with my soul, and with God.

Theo Androus, thank you for your friendship and passionate enthusiasm. You're one of my favorite human beings on this planet, and I'm so honored to have you as a friend. You've taught me so much about business, fatherhood, and life. Asa Siegel, my old-school homeboy! Through all the years, the miles, and the life changes, we've remained soul brothers. Thanks for your love and commitment. And thanks for always having my back.

John Brautovich, thank you for your wisdom, listening, love, and compassion. You carried me through the depths of this process and were there for me at every turn. Garrison Cohen, thank you for helping me manifest this dream and make it a reality. David Ferrera, I'm grateful for your love and for all that you did and still do to support me and my vision.

Johnny and Lara Fernandez, thank you for being such great friends. I am deeply inspired by your work, the way you live your lives and love each other, and your incredible parenting. Thanks for believing in me and helping me get this book out to others. Sean Flikke, thank you for being you and for the way you impact my life. Your friendship, your love, and your support mean so much to me.

Paul Foster, Jennifer Wenzel, Seth Schwartz, Carol Hartland, Muna Farhat, Mike Onorato, Erik Thrasher, Erin Moy, Natalie Lin, Karen Warner, Michele Jones, Sophia Ho, and the rest of the great team at Jossey-Bass and Wiley who worked so diligently in the creation of this book—thank you for your time, effort, and commitment.

To all of those I didn't mention specifically—friends, family members, clients, colleagues, coaches, mentors, speakers, authors, teachers, teams, organizations, and others who've supported me with this book, along my path, and in my life—thank you for encouraging me, challenging me, teaching me, being there for me, and helping bring out the best in me.

Finally, as a way of practicing what I preach, I appreciate myself. For the courage it took; for the many rejections and enormous amount of feedback I've endured over the past five years; for my willingness to learn and grow; for my vision, passion, and commitment; and for the vulnerability it takes to put myself out there like this, I honor and acknowledge myself.

focus on the good stuff

introduction

M any of us are walking around in a dark cloud of negativity. We focus much of our attention on the most stressful aspects of our lives, the things we don't like about others, and our own perceived weaknesses. To make matters worse, we live in a culture that has an obsession with the "bad stuff."

- Television news broadcasters assault us with story after story of violence, war, and fear. Even programs designed to entertain seem obsessed with negativity; by age eighteen the average person has already seen 200,000 violent acts on television, including 16,000 murders. The Internet, podcasts, print magazines, and other media likewise barrage us with bad news. "If it bleeds, it leads" is the mantra.
- Advertisers constantly remind us that we're not beautiful enough, strong enough, or fashionable enough. There's so much more we need to buy, but we'll never have enough stuff to be perfect; there's always more.
- Each of us deals every day with what we perceive to be negative aspects of our relationships with partners and

children, with our families, and in our situation at the workplace with coworkers and bosses.

- Many of us are concerned about the intense economic competition we face today. Millions of layoffs and rising costs have made our private lives a constant scramble for the resources we need to nourish our families and ourselves.

- Most of us obsess about our shortcomings and problems in such a disproportionate way that we end up feeling flawed, as though there were something wrong with us. We're hypercritical of ourselves.

This pervasive environment of negativity often causes us, as well as our families, groups, teams, and organizations, to focus on the bad stuff. As we breathe in this atmosphere of alarming news reports, fear-based commercials, and scary statistics, as well as the complaints, gossip, and frustration of the people around us, we tend to turn this negativity against others in the form of judgments or against ourselves as self-criticism. Collectively—in business, within families, and among communities—we seem to focus a great deal on problems, issues, and complaints.

In *Focus on the Good Stuff*, I'll show you how to move beyond this cycle of negativity, to focus on what *is* working and what you appreciate about yourself, others, and the world around you.

This book offers simple, effective, and powerful ways to raise your levels of appreciation, gratitude, and fulfillment, teaching you to dispel this culture of negativity and its cloud over your life. By reading this book, engaging in its exercises, and practicing the suggested tips and techniques, you'll begin to move beyond negativity and to harness the incredible power of appreciation. Focusing on the good stuff in a genuine way allows you to improve your relationships, create greater success and fulfillment, and experience a deep sense of gratitude for yourself, for others, and for life.

Don't Put Off Being Happy

Have you ever found yourself waiting for something "good" to happen so that you could be stress free and happy? "When I fall in love [get that promotion, lose those ten pounds, graduate from school, pay off my debt, have a baby, buy a house, accomplish that big goal, get to retirement . . .], I'll be happy!"

Sound familiar?

Many of us think like this all the time. But it never quite works out, does it? Either we do accomplish our goal, only to find out that in and of itself the accomplishment didn't make us genuinely happy, or we don't achieve what we're after, and we use our failure as evidence for our unhappiness. It's a classic lose-lose situation.

Having goals and pursuing them is a wonderfully important and exciting aspect of life and growth. Goals are essential to our ability to create success. However, we must remember that fulfillment and happiness come from a deep sense of appreciation and gratitude, not from achievement. Even our biggest accomplishments are meaningless if we don't appreciate them and appreciate ourselves in the process.

Underneath every dream or goal we have is a desire for appreciation. We want to feel good about ourselves and our lives. *Focus on the Good Stuff* is about getting to this deeper level of appreciation, which is what each of us is truly after. From my own life experience and from working with thousands of people over the past seven years as a motivational speaker, seminar leader, and personal coach, I've learned that appreciation is the *most important* aspect of fulfillment and happiness. It's the key to *real* success.

My Story

On Thursday, June 5, 1997, in the middle of my third season as a minor league player in the Kansas City Royals organization, I blew out my elbow and threw my last pitch as a professional baseball player. I was twenty-three years old. As a result of my injury, the next Sunday morning found me sitting on the floor of our locker room early in the morning before our game soaking my left elbow in a bucket of ice. Soon, some of my teammates came in and sat down on the couches close to me.

I was confused, and wondered what all of them were doing there so many hours before the game. Then I remembered that these guys were coming to participate in "baseball chapel," a short bible study and prayer service led by a local minister a few hours prior to our game each Sunday. Baseball chapel was optional and somewhat informal, but many players attended regularly. I sometimes went, not really out of any devout religious faith, but because it was a break from the monotony of the activities and conversations that went on every day at the ballpark.

That morning there was little choice; I was sitting there on the floor in the middle of the clubhouse, and the trainer had told me not to move my arm while icing it. Furthermore, I couldn't really get up and leave without disrupting what was about to take place. I stayed where I was. I was annoyed and definitely not interested in listening to this minister preach to us.

As he began to talk, I ignored him. Instead, I focused on the pain in my arm and the anxiety I felt about it. I'd been dealing with arm injuries since I was seventeen, but this one felt different. An appointment with the team doctor was scheduled for the following day, and way deep down in my gut I feared the worst: my baseball career was going to be over.

After the first few moments of chapel, however, the minister's story got my attention. Despite myself, I actually began to listen to him. The story he was telling took place many years ago and was about a young baseball player who was said to be phenomenally talented. At the tender age of only nineteen he'd made it all the way to the major leagues. That season, his very first in the majors, the young ball player struggled mightily. By the end of the first month he could no longer stand it; he walked into his manager's office and quit. He said baseball was no longer fun for him. He was frustrated because the fans were booing him, the newspaper reporters were writing negative things about him, and he couldn't hit a curve ball to save his life. He wanted to go home.

His manager looked at him, put an arm around his shoulder, and told him that he understood. He realized that the young man was frustrated and was uncomfortable facing public failure—and the resulting ridicule—for probably the first time in his life.

The manager said, "I know it's no fun to fail. But this game is hard, and sometimes you struggle. One of the hardest parts of playing baseball is that it's done publicly. When you fail, people see it, talk about it, and write about it. I know how difficult that can be. Unfortunately, it goes with the territory. Hang in there. You have the talent, son; you just have to believe in yourself. I believe in you. You can be a star here in the big leagues."

The ball player listened to his manager, whom he respected, and accepted his praise. He decided he would stay with it for the rest of the season. He went back out and began to improve. He started to hit those curve balls, and by and by the newspaper reporters began to write some positive things about his game. By the end of the season he was playing pretty well. He decided to come back and play again the following year.

The minister paused for a moment and looked around the locker room at each of us sitting there. Slowly and dramatically he said, "And Willie Mays went on to become one of the greatest players of all time."

Then the minister asked us, "What if Willie Mays had quit? What if he'd given up and given in to his fears and doubts? We would have lost not only one of the greatest baseball players that ever lived but also an American icon."

The part of his story that resonated most with me was that even though we all fail, we all worry, and we all have times we want to quit, there is an incredible amount of power when we have the courage to believe in ourselves and appreciate our gifts and talents. Sometimes we just need a nudge in a positive direction, like the one Mays got from his manager.

Listening to this story, so many emotions welled up inside me. Right there, in the middle of the clubhouse with my teammates around me, I began to cry. I felt embarrassed. Crying in the locker room was definitely not cool, but I couldn't control myself. These tears flowed because I could relate completely with how Willie Mays felt when he wanted to quit.

Moreover, it hit me that in my effort to be a great ball player all these years, I'd rarely appreciated how good I already was. My focus was always on getting better. I was consumed with not being great enough, and beat myself up constantly. I'd been afraid my entire baseball career that I was not going to make it, instead of appreciating how far I'd come.

Seeing Things More Clearly

Thinking back at that moment in the locker room, I was reminded of many of my great baseball experiences. Playing Little League with my friends, making my hometown all-star team and going to the state championships, traveling all over California with my summer league team in high school, getting recruited to play baseball at Stanford University, playing in the World Championships for Team USA, getting drafted by the New York Yankees out of high school, battling back from injuries and surgery to pitch successfully in college, winning the Pac-10 conference championship, making it to the College World Series and pitching in front of a national television audience of millions on CBS, getting drafted and signing a contract with the Kansas City Royals, playing in my first professional baseball game, going to my first spring training, putting on a real major league uniform—and the list went on.

I'd overcome a great deal of adversity in both baseball and life. My dad wasn't around much while I was growing up, and my family didn't have a lot of money. Nevertheless, I'd done everything I could to create opportunities for myself in both school and in sports, while dealing with intense self-doubt and even episodes of clinical depression.

Through all these challenges, I'd always been able to perform at a high level on and off the field. Looking at my life and baseball career up to that point, I realized that there was so much for me to appreciate, but, sadly, I'd not been paying much attention to all this good stuff along the way.

Sitting in the clubhouse that morning, I finally recognized all that I'd accomplished and overcome. Even though I was staring the end of my baseball career in the face and realizing all that I'd missed along the way, in that moment I had a wonderful sense of appreciation for who I was and for what I'd accomplished, one that I'd never felt before. Yes, I felt scared and disappointed about the possibility of life without baseball, but my fears were swallowed up by my overwhelming feeling of pride.

As the morning passed and chapel ended, I realized that on a deeper level, the pride I felt was not even about my specific accomplishments, as great as they were; it was more about the courage, strength, and determination I'd demonstrated in persevering and making those things happen. I'd been so focused on my ultimate goal, on what needed improvement, on working hard, and on trying to do all the right things. My only fault was that I'd forgotten to enjoy myself along the way.

As I looked around the locker room that morning, I saw the faces of my fellow teammates. For the very first time in my baseball career I could actually see, feel, and understand their fear. They all had a big dream, just like me. They wanted to "make it." I could see in their eyes, though, that they were scared too. All that time I'd thought that I was the only one who felt that way.

We were so hard on ourselves. There we were, a group of healthy and talented young men getting paid to play the game we'd each loved since childhood. It should've been a dream come true for all of us. However, due to the intense pressure, stress, and expectation that were both self-imposed and perpetuated in that environment, most of us had little sense of appreciation for ourselves, each other, or the exciting opportunity of playing professional baseball.

Discovering Appreciation—A Life-Defining Moment

Through all the thoughts and emotions I experienced during that short time in the clubhouse that Sunday morning, I learned a great deal about myself and about life. I realized that if I could've put more attention on appreciating myself, my teammates, and my environment, I would've been able to enjoy the experience of playing baseball much more, and my chances of being successful and fulfilled would've greatly increased.

On a larger scale, I realized the importance of appreciation and how vital it is to true fulfillment and success in life. I didn't have to be dependent on my results to be able to truly appreciate myself, my life, and those around me. In that defining moment, I made a commitment to look for, see, and appreciate the greatness in myself and others all the time.

The End of My Baseball Career

This commitment stayed with me as I saw the doctor the following day and was sent back to California for a major operation on my arm. That following spring, before I was fully healed from my surgery, the Kansas City Royals released me from my contract. Still determined, I did everything I could to rehabilitate my arm and get back out on the mound. But after two more operations, hundreds of hours of physical therapy, and various forms of alternative medical treatments, it was clear to me that the pain in my arm would never allow me to pitch at a high enough level for my baseball career to continue.

On my twenty-fifth birthday, February 7, 1999, sitting at a restaurant with my family, I announced to them that I was retiring from baseball and moving on with my life. It was both sad and liberating at the same time. From the age of seven, up until that moment I'd known exactly what I wanted to do with my life, where I was headed, and what was most important to me.

As I looked back on my baseball career, I realized two really interesting things. First, the only regret I had from those eighteen years was that I had not fully appreciated myself and my experience while it was happening. Second, that day in the locker room, the story about Willie Mays that the minister told us and my insight about the importance of gratitude and appreciation, had been one of the highlights of my career and my life. I knew I wanted to focus my life, personally and ultimately professionally, on remembering this important lesson and reminding others of it as well.

Riding the Dot-Com Bubble and Discovering My True Calling

At this time in my life, I had no idea how I would achieve this new goal of living a life of gratitude and appreciation, and teaching others to do the same. After retiring from baseball, I began working in advertising sales and business development for an Internet start-up company. The dot-com boom was in full swing, and I was lucky to be riding that exciting bandwagon. At this same time, I got even more passionate about my own personal growth, which had always been important to me. I read lots of books, listened to tapes and CDs, and attended as many personal development seminars as I could find. I wanted to be happy, to learn about myself, and to figure out from a mental, emotional, and spiritual perspective what life was all about and how to be truly successful and fulfilled.

Through all of the books, tapes, and seminars, I kept hearing powerful messages about what I already knew to be true: that gratitude, appreciation, and self-love were the keys to ultimate success and fulfillment. I also found myself called to share my own story, my own insights, and my own wisdom with others in a way that would make a difference for them. Even though I worried that I was too young, that no one would listen to me, and that I didn't know what I was doing, I wanted to follow my heart and passion and start a business as a motivational speaker and life coach.

In July 2000, I got laid off from the new Internet start-up I'd just gone to work for. Yet again, I experienced a personal and powerful example of how I, and many of the people around me, didn't appreciate the blessings and success of something (in this case the dot-com boom) until it was over.

About a month before my company was scheduled to go public, with many of us anticipating a windfall of hundreds of thousands (if not millions) of dollars, it all came crashing to the ground. Actually, the layoff was a blessing, and it gave me the kick in the butt that I needed to launch into the work I truly wanted to do and have now been doing full time for the past seven years: empowering individuals and groups to focus on the good stuff, remember all that they're grateful for, and use the incredible power of appreciation to transform their lives.

My Work and Its Impact

Using my background in sports, my own personal experiences, and my years of studying personal development, psychology, and human development, I've had the privilege of working with thousands of people over these past seven years.

Through one-on-one coaching sessions, articles, public workshops, and hundreds of speaking engagements with such organizations as AT&T, the U.S. Department of Labor, New York Life Insurance, Kaiser Permanente, and many more, I've been teaching the powerful principles of appreciation and gratitude contained in this book for quite some time.

My clients and audience members have used these tips and techniques to improve their relationships, create greater success and fulfillment in their lives, and appreciate themselves and those close to them in a meaningful way. Over the years of work with my clients, I've seen

- Individuals expand the gratitude and appreciation they experience toward themselves and their lives, as well as in their relationships with others

- People resolve conflicts with their significant others, family members, friends, and coworkers
- Individuals gain confidence and clarity about their dreams and take effective actions toward the fulfillment of these goals
- People increase their productivity and success by focusing on their strengths and by being grateful for all they already have
- Teams and groups communicate more effectively and in an appreciative way
- Organizations transform their culture from one of negativity and gossip to one of appreciation and empowerment

By reading this book, focusing on the good stuff, and utilizing the power of appreciation, you'll be able to create these types of results in your own life and with the people around you. Appreciating yourself, others, and life is the most important thing you can do to transform your life, improve your relationships, and create the success and fulfillment that you truly want.

How to Use This Book

Focus on the Good Stuff is divided into three parts. Part One addresses the "problem" that has contributed to the epidemic of negativity in our culture, our relationships, and within ourselves. This problem is both complex and pervasive. Chapter One looks at the negativity that we have toward others and that exists all around us in our culture; Chapter Two focuses on the negativity that we have toward ourselves in the form of self-criticism.

For you to integrate and utilize the transformative power of appreciation in your life, it's essential that you take a real look at how pervasive this cultural and personal negativity is and how it affects you and the world around you. It's also essential to take an honest look at what makes appreciation for life, others, and yourself difficult or challenging on a personal level. Part One is designed to delve deeply into negativity and its impact on you.

Part Two focuses on the "solution." The five powerful principles of appreciation discussed in Part Two are ones that I've developed over my years of working with individuals and groups. They're each designed to empower you with new ideas, perspectives, and practices that lead to greater appreciation, success, and fulfillment in your life, your relationships, and your communities. Here they are:

Principle 1:   Be Grateful
Principle 2:   Choose Positive Thoughts and Feelings
Principle 3:   Use Positive Words
Principle 4:   Acknowledge Others
Principle 5:   Appreciate Yourself

These five principles of appreciation are all powerful concepts that I teach people in coaching sessions, as well as in my seminars, workshops, and keynote speeches. Each principle builds on the one before it, leading you through a process that starts with looking for the good stuff in life; addresses the power of your thoughts, feelings, and words; moves into finding the good in others and letting them know about it; and concludes with the most important and powerful aspect of all, appreciating and loving yourself. These principles are all simple to understand and implement. Putting them into practice in your life will have a remarkable impact on you, those around you, and your sense of success and fulfillment.

Part Three is all about action. Making lasting change in our lives is not so much about what we know, but what we do. This final section of the book allows you to integrate what you've read and learned, and come up with specific ways to put it into action in your life.

Interactive Exercises and Positive Practices

Nearly every chapter includes interactive exercises for you to do as you go along. Each exercise is designed to be done in the moment, as you read it. The exercises allow you to engage with the material in a personal and specific way that is unique to you and your life.

At the end of most of the chapters I describe several "positive practices." Each suggested practice is usable, practical, and detailed. They are designed to have you actually practice the lessons of each principle of appreciation in your daily life. I've listed a variety of these practices so as to give you many options to choose from or to spark your own unique ideas for other practices that could work for you. Although you're welcome to use them all, the best approach is to pick one or two of your favorites and start using them in your life as you are reading the book. You also may want to jot them down or talk about them with others as a way of keeping them fresh in your mind.

All these exercises and practices are ones I use myself and with my clients. They are "road tested" and designed to raise your levels of appreciation and gratitude. Some of these exercises and practices are focused on you as an individual; in other words, you can do them by yourself as you read through the book. Others are designed to do with a partner (husband, wife, friend, family member, significant other) or with a group (work team, sports team, family, community group, and so on). It's a good idea for you to have a journal or notebook handy as you read through the book so that you will have an organized place to write, make lists, and fully engage in these exercises and practices. Have fun with them and remember they're just "practices," so you can't mess them up.

As a speaker, seminar leader, and coach, I've worked with thousands of people from all walks of life. In my own life, I practice these principles of appreciation and gratitude on a daily basis. As I see day in and day out in my work with others and in my personal life, it is our ability to feel and express true appreciation and to focus on the good stuff that leads to genuine fulfillment in our lives, not the other way around. The art of appreciating our lives is much more than simply saying thank you or noticing nice things around us from time to time. True appreciation is about completely altering the way we relate to ourselves, others, and the world around us. By committing ourselves to living a life of appreciation and gratitude, we put ourselves on a true path of deep fulfillment and authentic happiness.

Thanks for picking up this book and joining me on this journey. Once you're finished, I hope you'll let me know what you think and share some of your own ideas by writing me at mike@mike-robbins.com. But first, let's get started.

part one

∞

our obsession with bad stuff

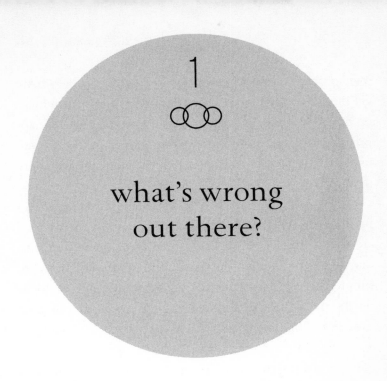

1

what's wrong
out there?

Negativity is pervasive in our world today, as you will readily see if you go online, turn on your television, pick up a newspaper, or listen to the daily conversations that take place around you. On a personal level, think about your own negative thoughts, feelings, and conversations with others, and the challenges, issues, and conflicts in your life that you worry about.

If you stop and pay attention, much of what we see, say, hear, think about, and witness is focused on "bad stuff." We love to talk about what's wrong, to gossip about the faults or apparent misdeeds of others, to obsess about our own problems, and to complain in general. So before we get into the principles of appreciation that allow us to focus on the good stuff—as a way to create a greater sense of happiness, peace, and fulfillment in our lives and those around us—we have to take an honest look at the insidious nature of negativity.

Appreciating ourselves, acknowledging others, and focusing on what we're grateful for, in and of themselves, are pretty simple. We all know how to do these things to one degree or another. However, although these actions are simple, they are not so easy to do given how much we focus on the most stressful and challenging aspects of our own lives and of life in general.

On both a cultural and personal level we tend to place a disproportionate amount of our attention and energy on what we perceive as bad or wrong. Why do we do this? The answer to this question is complex. We'll look at the first part of the answer here in Chapter One; Chapter Two discusses the second and more personal aspect of this answer.

In this chapter we'll look at some of ways negativity shows up in our lives, our relationships, and the world around us. It's important for us to start here, because as we confront our own negativity in an honest way, we're actually able to deal with it effectively and then move beyond it. Looking at our negativity directly and owning it is the first step in transforming it.

Our Obsession with Our Problems

So many of us are obsessed with the problems, issues, and conflicts in our lives. We often love to talk about the challenges we have at work, in our relationships, with our children, and more. Think about much of what gets talked about when we get together with our family members or good friends. Whether it's health issues, conflicts with others, financial challenges, political issues, or complaints about life, other people, or ourselves—we tend to focus a lot of attention and energy on our difficulties.

Even people who aren't comfortable talking about some of these things out loud will often think about and worry about their problems, issues, and stresses. One of my coaching clients, Sherry, said, "Mike, I hate to talk about my problems—like the things I hate about my boss, the challenges I have with my husband, or the fact that both of my kids are getting in trouble at school these days. However, I can't stop thinking about these issues. I have dreams about them, worry about them, and find that they dominate my life each day."

Thinking about and talking about our problems, issues, and challenges can be very positive and productive for us to do. However, the process is positive only if our thoughts and conversations about our difficulties help us move through the negativity, make positive changes, and let go. Most of the time, however, we simply obsess about our problems, which makes them worse. This obsession leads to more negativity and problems, which ultimately have a debilitating impact on our lives.

Negativity Toward Others

If you spent an entire day monitoring your thoughts and conversations, how much of what you think and say about other people would be critical?

Although the answer to this question will vary for each of us, sadly much of what we think and say about other people is negative. We tend to focus on what we don't like, what gets on our nerves, or what annoys us about other people. If you walk into a conversation that's already going on about a person who is not present, the conversation will often be one of criticism, judgment, or gossip.

Why is this, and what impact does this negativity have on us, our relationships, and our environments? There are a variety of reasons that this occurs and a myriad of impacts that this interpersonal criticalness has on us. The bottom line is that it's pervasive, and it gets in the way of our ability to express any real appreciation or gratitude for the people around us. Let's look at some of the ways this negativity manifests itself in our daily lives and why appreciation of others can be difficult or challenging for many of us.

Judgments

Have you ever noticed how many judgmental thoughts you have? We have opinions about everyone and everything.

Most of them we don't even have to think about. My brain can be like an automatic judgment machine if I'm not careful: "I don't like that, I don't agree with that, that's stupid, she's weird, he's ugly, what's wrong with him, why does she eat like that, what's he wearing, I hate people who drive like that, she's too pushy, he's too aggressive, that guy needs to lose a few pounds, what happened to her face, why is he so arrogant, calm down," and on and on and on.

These judgmental thoughts come and go all day long for most of us. The problem is not only the thoughts themselves but that we think they are "true." Many of us have a hard time distinguishing between our opinions and the truth. Just because we think something is right or wrong doesn't make it so. I know this is a simple concept, but many of us forget it, and we continue to believe that our opinions are facts.

Given the negative nature of our culture, our obsessive focus on the bad stuff, and the encouragement—direct or indirect—to think about and talk about the things and people we don't like, many of us are stuck in a trap of negative and judgmental thinking all the time. The worst part about it is that we often don't even notice our judgments; we don't realize they're running our life and coloring our experience of everyone and everything. It's like when the air conditioner is on and making lots of noise, but we can't hear it because we've gotten used to it. It's only when it shuts off and gets really quiet that we are able to realize how loud it was in the first place.

Our judgments and opinions have a huge impact on our life, the way we see things, and our relationships. For example, imagine that you have a strongly negative opinion of the president, which many people do, regardless of which president it is. You and your negative, judgmental opinion may sit down to watch the State of the Union address on TV. Given your feelings about the president, what do you think your impression of the speech will be? Most likely, you'll pay attention to all the things you don't like, don't agree with, and think are stupid about the speech, the ideas presented, and the president himself (or someday soon, herself).

Someone else watching the same speech with a more positive opinion of the president will probably have a different experience and come to a very different conclusion. The speech is the same in either case, but our judgments of the person delivering the speech have a huge impact on how we perceive it.

This same phenomenon holds true with our loved ones, friends, family, coworkers, and others. Our opinions and judgments determine how we see them. In other words, we always find what we look for. Sadly, we're often looking for what we don't like.

There's nothing wrong with our having opinions about things and people—we all do and we always will. The problem isn't with our opinions themselves; it's the attitude of righteous judgment that we attach to them—thinking we are Right with a capital "R" about all our assessments. And given that many of us have a tendency to focus our attention on the things that we don't like about other people, we paint ourselves into a negative corner with our limiting judgments.

Gossip

Many of us love to gossip—talking about someone else in a hushed, secretive tone; repeating bad things we've heard that may or may not be true; and enjoying it, laughing about it, chortling together with other like-minded folks. On a cultural level, we see this all over the place. There are TV shows, magazines, and newspaper articles devoted to gossip. On a personal level, we all know someone (or many people) who love to talk about the "dirt" on everyone else. Let's be honest: some of us know that *we* are that person.

Gossip really falls into two categories—our negative mental judgments about others spoken out loud, and the retelling of negative stories or rumors about someone else. Either way, we see, hear, and participate in gossip all the time.

When I was fourteen I got my first job as a busboy at the Mexican restaurant up the street from my house in Oakland, California. It was a big deal for me, and I was excited to be making some money for myself. I wanted to buy a car when I turned sixteen, and this job was my ticket. I remember being a bit overwhelmed by the training process—lots of details to learn and things to take care of.

The head busboy, in charge of training me, was a seventeen-year-old guy named Pete. Pete had been there for over a year, was a senior in high school (I was just a freshman at the time), and seemed to have the whole place figured out. I looked up to him and was glad he was showing me the ropes. On my very first night of training, I followed him around, and he told me all the things I needed to do and learn to be successful in the job—clean off the plates, set up the tables with glasses and silverware, bring chips and water to the new tables, and so on.

On our first break, Pete took me out back and started telling me all kinds of things about the other people who worked in the restaurant—the managers, waiters and waitresses, other busboys and busgirls, cooks, bartenders, hostesses, and even dish washers. Some of these people I'd already met that night, but many of them I had not. He told me who was cool, who was mean, who was weird, who was having sex with whom, who drank too much, who was good at their job, who wasn't, and all kinds of other juicy details. I loved it and really appreciated his giving me all this inside information about everyone else.

I now call this the "off the record" training. This is the part of the training process that we get at almost every job, where someone or a group of people "downloads" all the gossip—all the dirt about our coworkers or teammates and also many of the informant's judgmental opinions.

If you've ever worked for an organization, joined a group of any kind, or started a new job, you know exactly what I'm talking about. When I mention this example in the keynotes and seminars I deliver for organizations, it always gets a huge laugh of recognition. It's a very real and specific example of gossip and how it shows up in groups.

Although gossip may seem harmless, it's ultimately one of the biggest issues that divide groups. I believe that gossip to an organization is like cancer to the body; it slowly eats away at the fabric of the team until the team itself dies.

In families and personal relationships, gossip is equally as harmful. We may all have a "crazy" uncle, or someone who we think talks too much, eats too much, or wears funny clothes at our family functions. However, when we share our negative opinions about our family members to our friends and other family members, we actually make things worse.

Comparison and Competition

Competition is another significant cause of negativity toward others. Whether or not you consider yourself to be very competitive, we live in an extremely competitive society, and since we were little most of us have been taught—directly or indirectly—to compare ourselves to others and compete with our siblings, our friends, our classmates, and our teammates. We learned to believe that if we could run faster, get better grades, jump higher, or play music better, or if we were taller, prettier, stronger, then we'd be able to win, succeed, and be happier for the rest of our lives.

Well, as we all know, this "training" didn't pay off or really hold true. Comparison and competition don't help us be more successful or happy—in many cases, just the opposite is true.

One of the most intense examples of comparison and competition I ever experienced was my very first spring training with the Kansas City Royals. I signed my pro baseball contract with the Royals in June 1995 at the age of twenty-one. I came to spring training that next March feeling pretty good about myself, confident in my ability, and excited about my first full season of professional baseball. Getting to the spring training facility the morning before our first workout was very exciting for me. In my locker hung an actual Kansas City Royals big league uniform. It was a few years old and was no longer being used by the big leaguers, but it was the real deal. And on the back it said ROBBINS in big, bold letters. I was excited!

We were told to meet on the practice field for a full-group meeting. The group was made up of just pitchers and catchers—we had to report to camp a few days early to get our arms ready and in shape before the rest of the guys got there. All of us pitchers were in white uniforms, and all of the catchers were wearing blue uniform tops with gray pants. It was easy to tell us apart.

As the meeting began and some of the coaches started talking to us, I noticed that my attention moved away from the meeting and on to the group. I was amazed by the large number of players there. I didn't know most of these guys, but many of them looked like "studs" to me. (Stud in baseball jargon is used to describe a really good and talented player.)

My curiosity and competitive nature kicked in, and I decided to count how many pitchers were at that meeting with me. I counted seventy-five. I couldn't believe there were that many, so I counted again. Yep, seventy-five pitchers, just in minor league camp. And they told us that there were another twenty-five pitchers "across the street" (at major league camp).

I'd been in many competitive baseball environments up to that point in my life and career, but none had been quite like this. This was for real—this was pro baseball, and my dream and future were on the line. As our spring training games started, I noticed that I was rooting against the other pitchers. I didn't do it overtly, but underneath my positive exterior, I would laugh when someone pitched badly, and there was even a part of me that got embarrassingly excited when someone got cut or even hurt. Each time that happened, I knew that there was one less pitcher for me to compete against. It was sick, but true. That environment, coupled with my intense desire to win and succeed, turned me into a comparing, competitive monster.

Many of us are quite proud of our competitiveness and our drive to succeed. We have, unfortunately, confused competition with success. Wanting to succeed, pushing ourselves, and enjoying winning are wonderful things. Wanting to beat others, wishing bad things on our competition, and critically comparing ourselves to other people can be damaging, negative, and hurtful. When we relate to others from this place of comparison and competition, someone has to win and someone has to lose. This naturally sets up a negative dynamic that makes appreciation, acknowledgment, and gratitude difficult, if not impossible.

Lack of Appreciation

Whereas judgments, gossip, comparison, and competition can be overt forms of interpersonal negativity, lack of appreciation is more subtle, but it's just as pervasive and has a huge impact.

The U.S. Department of Labor came out with some statistics a few years ago that cited the top reasons why people in the United States choose to leave their jobs. *The number one reason cited in the survey was lack of appreciation.* Of the people who leave their jobs, 64 percent say they do so because they don't feel appreciated or valued. According to Gallup, 65 percent of people in the United States say that they receive no praise or recognition in the workplace.

On a more personal level, most of the fights, arguments, and disagreements we have with our friends, coworkers, family members, and especially with our significant others come down to one fundamental issue: one or both of us isn't feeling appreciated. Lack of appreciation is the source of most of the problems and issues we face in our relationships, and it is a key aspect of interpersonal negativity.

A client of mine named Susan came to me to work on her relationships with other people, specifically her husband, Jim. She told me that over the past few years she and Jim seemed to be growing apart and that the excitement, passion, and love she'd felt in the early years of her marriage were starting to die out. She was sad, scared, and angry about it, but didn't know what to do.

Susan was a self-admitted "good girl" who avoided confrontation, arguments, or disagreements of any kind. She and Jim didn't fight, and they weren't overtly hostile to one another at all. He worked a lot, and when he wasn't working, he spent time doing projects around the house, taking their kids to activities, and coaching soccer. Susan said that even though she wasn't very happy with him, Jim was a "good man, husband, and father."

As we talked further about it, what became clear was that Susan no longer felt adored, appreciated, or cherished by Jim as she had when they first got married. It had actually been many years since she'd felt that way, and it wasn't until now that she discovered it was the lack of appreciation that was causing her feelings of disconnection from Jim.

When she looked deeper, Susan was also able to see that she had stopped appreciating Jim. Although given her personality she wasn't overtly critical of him, she acknowledged that she rarely complimented him or expressed her love and appreciation in any demonstrative way anymore. She said that because she hadn't been feeling close or excited about him and their marriage, she didn't want to send the wrong message and have him think that things were going well when they clearly weren't, in her opinion. Through our coaching sessions Susan realized that she had pulled back and was withholding her appreciation.

Susan and Jim are not unique; this is what happens in many relationships. We forget—accidentally or on purpose—to acknowledge and appreciate our significant other, and it leads to resentment, disconnection, and pain for one or both of us. Whenever my wife, Michelle, gets upset with me, I know that somewhere behind her frustration, anger, or sadness is a feeling of a lack of appreciation.

Think of your relationships, both the ones you consider "good" and especially the ones you consider "bad." If you look at them closely, you'll probably see that there's a lack of appreciation on your part or on the part of the other person. You're likely to find that the lack of appreciation is the real issue, not whatever specific thing you have been focusing on.

Justifying Our Negativity Toward Others

We have rationalizations for all our judgments and even for our gossip and competition with others. It's all about them, those other people. If they didn't do those annoying things, we wouldn't have to judge them, make them wrong, or talk about them, right?

We're obsessed with being right at all costs. Have you ever been in an argument with someone, and right in the middle of it realized that the other person was actually right and you were wrong? I know that for me this can be a humbling and humiliating experience. Oftentimes I've actually continued to argue even though I knew I was wrong, simply out of pure pride, ego, or spite. I'm sure you can relate to this in one way or another.

Sometimes our justifications for being critical or negative toward others are even more "noble" than arrogant righteousness. I was hired by the owner of a big apartment building to coach the manager who ran the day-to-day operations of his building. The owner had been getting a lot of negative feedback about this manager, Bradley. Many of his employees and tenants felt that he was too gruff, cold, and critical.

When Bradley and I first met to discuss the situation, he told me, "I'm not here to be nobody's friend. Each person in this building is either someone who gets a paycheck from me or someone who pays me rent. They ain't going to like me no matter what, so why bother wasting my time kissing their butts or being nice to them?"

It was obvious how with that kind of attitude, Bradley was rubbing people the wrong way. He clearly felt justified in his attitude and actions as he told me all about his past employees who had done bad things and the tenants he'd evicted for various dramatic reasons, and all of his justifications made sense to me. However, what Bradley couldn't see was that his lack of appreciation and his overt criticalness were actually contributing to the problems and to the tension that everyone felt in the building. Even though he felt justifiably victimized by his "bad" employees and tenants, Bradley was actually participating in and creating greater negativity through his attitude and expectations.

After a few months of our working together, Bradley began to see that his attitude toward the people around him was contributing to the negative situation in his building. As he was able to alter his approach and perspective toward others, things began to change in a positive way.

Like Bradley, many of us blame other people for our judgments, instead of taking responsibility for our opinions, addressing difficult situations directly, and dealing with people up front when we have an issue or a problem with them. We think people should speak, act, and think the same way we do. When they don't, we feel justified in our self-righteous judgments, gossip, criticism, and negativity toward them.

The Impact of Our Negativity

So how do our obsessions with our problems, judgments, gossip, comparisons, competition, lack of appreciation, and justifications affect our lives? This is an important question for us to ask and to answer honestly in our journey of growth and discovery. The answer to this question varies for each of us.

Suffice it to say, your negativity has a major impact on you to the degree that you engage in these patterns of thought, feeling, and behavior. In other words, the more you do these negative things, the more they affect you, those around you, and your relationships with them.

It's very difficult to have meaningful, loving relationships with people whom we judge, criticize, and gossip about all the time. It is virtually impossible to empower or inspire people if we make them wrong. As Dr. Martin Luther King Jr. insightfully said, "We have no morally persuasive power with those who can feel our underlying contempt for them."

It's essential for you to be honest with yourself about your own interpersonal negativity. We all engage in this to some degree or another. When we can bring our negativity toward others into the light, tell the truth about it, and look at the impact it has on us and those around us, then we can start to do something to alter it.

Being honest and truly facing our negativity allows us to deal with it and is the first essential step we must take in moving beyond it. If our negativity stays unconscious or if we continue to feel righteously justified about it, then it becomes dangerous and very damaging. Don't beat yourself up about this, but simply notice it.

Questions to Ponder About Your Negativity

The following questions are intended to make this issue more real and specific for you and your life. Think about them or write down your answers in a journal or on a piece of paper.

1. Which type or types of negativity (obsession with problems, judgments, gossip, comparison, competition, or lack of appreciation) are your "favorites"?
2. What impact does this negativity have on you and your relationships?
3. Which of your negative opinions are you willing to "poke holes" in for the purpose of seeing other and possibly more positive perspectives?

If you're not sure about the answers to any of these questions, I encourage you to ask some of your close friends, your family members, or your significant other. If you ask them to be totally honest with you, they'll probably have very specific and enlightening feedback that will help you see how your own interpersonal negativity affects your life, your relationships, and them in particular.

The Culture of Negativity

In addition to our obsession with our own problems and our negativity toward others, we also must acknowledge the enormous amount of negativity that exists within our culture and its impact on us. Although cultural negativity may seem like it's "out there," our outside world is just a reflection of our inner world, a mirror. Everything going on around us has an impact and has to do with our personal journey. There are many ways cultural negativity manifests itself. Let's take a look at just a few specific examples of the negativity that shows up around us and how the "external" messages we hear and see in our society have a personal impact on us.

Violence and Scandals

The news media—on television, radio, and in print—are dominated by stories of violence, scandal, and negativity. These stories are "sexy." They sell newspapers and magazines, lure us into going online, make us tune in and watch, and get us talking. In today's world of ever-expanding twenty-four-hour cable news, political talk radio, and Internet bloggers, the competition by the media and the focus on "shock value," controversy, and negativity seem more intense than ever.

Think of some of the top news stories of the past decade or so—the O. J. Simpson murder trial, the Bill Clinton–Monica Lewinsky affair and subsequent impeachment hearing, the 2000 presidential election, the steroid scandal in baseball, the Laci Peterson murder, the Enron scandal, 9/11, Hurricane Katrina, just to name a few. I'm not saying that these stories weren't important to report. However, the degree to which they were covered by the media and the insatiable nature of some people's desire for information about these stories were completely out of proportion to their intrinsic value and importance in our lives.

Here are two fascinating statistics that exemplify the media's increased obsession with negativity and violence. Between 1990 and 1998, the murder rate in the United States decreased by 20 percent. During that same period, the number of stories about murder on network newscasts increased by 600 percent.

When there's a terrible accident, murder, kidnapping, school shooting, violent storm, public argument between celebrities, or other act of violence or scandal, the media consider it to be top news.

There is, of course, a certain amount of genuinely disturbing information that is important to hear about—a war, a downturn in the economy, a storm warning, or other bad news that we need to know. The overall result of these negative messages, however, is that anyone tuning in or reading various news sources can get the impression that the world is in a perpetual crisis and that everything is terrible everywhere.

Meanwhile, there is all kinds of good stuff going on in the world. Every day, people wake up, go to work, and do their best to be loving, useful, selfless, loyal, and devoted to their loved ones, families, work, friends, and community. But sadly we rarely see anything about this in the media.

The Culture of Fear

Barry Glassner, a sociology professor at USC and the author of the best-selling book The Culture of Fear, says that "In the U.S., our fears are so exaggerated and out of control that anxiety is the number-one mental health problem in the country." He points out that much of what we're taught to fear in our culture is actually unfounded and not even based on real statistics or research.

Glassner believes that we're often manipulated by politicians, advocacy groups, marketers, the news media, and others who have specific agendas and are highly skilled at tapping into our primal fears in order to get us to do what they want us to do (vote for them, support their cause, buy their products, or watch their shows).

Whether you fully agree with Glassner's theory or not, it's clear that we live in a world filled with messages of fear. Think for a moment about all the things we are encouraged to fear—terrorism, economic uncertainty, violence, illness, pesticides, global warming, cholesterol, carbohydrates, criminals, anthrax, aging, and drunk drivers—just to name a few. If we actually made a list of all the things we've been told to "watch out for" by our friends, teachers, coworkers, and family members, as well as everything we've read, heard, and seen through the media, it would make our heads spin.

Constant Complaining

Do you know people who love to complain? You may actually know them really well. One of them may be sitting in your chair right now! Many of us get off on complaining.

People will often strike up conversations with total strangers and say something like, "Can you believe this awful weather we're having? When is this annoying rain going to stop?" It is socially acceptable and totally expected that people are going to get together and commiserate with one another about problems, issues, and complaints.

In the business world, complaining is rampant. When I speak to corporate groups about this issue, almost everyone agrees that there's an enormous amount of complaining that goes on within their organization. People complain about their management, fellow employees, workload, benefits, pressure, politics, other departments, clients, the industry, the economy—you name it.

Think for a moment of all the things you and those around you complain about—gas prices, traffic, crime, weather, youth, politicians, media, entertainment, food, parking, other people, and so much more. Have you noticed that most of what we complain about doesn't actually get any better? Even the act of complaining, which some of us call "venting," rarely makes us feel good; it just contributes to more complaining and more negativity. Ultimately, these complaints lead to the deeper problem of cynicism.

Cynicism

Have you ever been made fun of for being too happy? This has happened to me thousands of times throughout my life. I've always found it to be quite strange. Why would we make fun of other people for being too happy? Isn't happiness what most of us are striving for in life?

I often hear people ask in a cynical tone, "What are you so happy about this morning? What did you put in your coffee?" There seems to be some unwritten rule in our society that you aren't allowed to be too happy, or there must be something wrong with you. There are two quotations that come to mind that speak to this point.

In the hilarious movie *The Princess Bride*, Westley (the hero) says to his love, Princess Buttercup (while he's still hiding behind his disguise as the "Dread Pirate Roberts" and she doesn't yet know his real identity), "Life is pain, Highness; anyone who says otherwise is selling something."

On the great TV show *Cheers*, one of my favorite characters of all time, Norm, has a classic line as he strolls into the bar in one particular episode. He comes in and says his usual, "Afternoon everybody," to which the crowd in the bar replies with its customary, "NORM!" As Norm makes his way to his personal bar stool, Woody asks him, "How's it going today, Mr. Peterson?" Norm replies, in his classic dead-pan way, "Woody, it's a dog-eat-dog world out there, and I'm wearing Milk Bone underwear."

Even though our fictional friend Norm is saying this on a sitcom to get a laugh, sadly his joke reflects an attitude and perspective shared by many in our culture. This speaks to the cynical nature of our collective thinking. Many people actually live their lives as if other people were out to get them.

Cynicism kills ideas, teamwork, possibilities, hope, and definitely appreciation. It damages relationships, breaks up organizations, and leads to conflicts of all kinds. Think about the cynicism that exists around you—at work, at home, and in general. Often we don't even notice it because it has become so commonplace in our culture.

Cynicism is a product of our negative focus and obsession. It's seen as cool, hip, and even sophisticated to be cynical. Open, happy, positive people, groups, and organizations are often seen as naïve dreamers, as unrealistic or "Pollyanna."

Negative Ads

Over the past few decades we've seen a major increase in the use of attack ads in political campaigns. Although many people are outspoken about their dislike of these negative ads, the reality is that the candidates continue to run them because they work—or at least so we're told by the "experts."

If we look at other forms of advertising, we see that it's not only the politicians who use negative ads to defeat the competition and sell themselves. Fear, pain, and negativity are used all day, every day by Madison Avenue and companies selling a variety of products. We're bombarded with images and messages telling us what's wrong with us, what we should watch out for, and that if we don't buy this particular product we'll be doomed. These ads often denigrate the competition and put down other products that are pretty much the same as the one they are promoting.

If you watch TV for an entire day and flip through a few magazines from time to time, you'll see ads for hair loss products, teeth-whitening solution, weight loss pills, depression medication, exercise machines, makeup, skin care products, and much more. All these ads are aimed directly at our fears and insecurities. And they work. We all have been influenced by these ads, have purchased some of these products (whether or not we needed them), or at least have been left with a negative feeling about ourselves or about life.

The Blame Game

We live in a culture that is full of blame. There are examples of it everywhere. The number of lawsuits continues to rise. People are suing each other left and right. Democrats blame Republicans; Republicans blame Democrats. Environmentalists blame big business; big business blames environmental activists. Workers blame management; management blames workers. Men blame women; women blame men. Children (of all ages) blame their parents, and parents blame their kids. On and on it goes.

A sad example of the blame game occurred in the aftermath of Hurricane Katrina. Katrina was described by many as one of the worst and most devastating natural disasters in the history of our country. Thousands of lives were lost, and damage in the billions of dollars was incurred. For most of us sitting at home watching the events unfold on television, the days that followed the hurricane were scary, sad, and difficult to witness. The people displaced by the hurricane, especially those in New Orleans, were left without food, water, shelter, or much support. Many people in the news media, as well as outspoken advocates, politicians, and community leaders, began immediately calling for support and passionately criticizing the government—local, state, and national—for its lack of response.

By most accounts, the response time was slow, and the relief effort was not well planned or executed. However, as the dust began to settle, it seemed clear that no one was willing to step up and take responsibility for what happened. The mayor blamed the president; the president blamed the mayor and governor; politicians were pointing fingers to other politicians, agencies, and even to the citizens who did not evacuate or follow the prestorm recommendations. All in all, a tragic situation was made worse by the fact that none of the leaders involved were willing to admit any fault or take responsibility for what happened.

Whether we're politicians, corporate executives, celebrities, professional athletes, or just regular people, we're encouraged, trained, and coached (directly or indirectly) in our society to deny, blame, and point fingers. There seems to be yet another unwritten rule in our culture that says, "Don't take responsibility unless you get caught or absolutely have to." This blame game is everywhere and has a big cost.

The more personal reason that the blame game exists is that it's much easier for us to blame others, society, and the world than it is for us to take responsibility for our own lives and our own happiness.

The Impact of Cultural Negativity

So how does all this cultural negativity affect us? The answer isn't simple or easy, and it's different for each of us. We all feel the impact in a variety of unique ways:

- Some of us can't stand the place we work because it's so critical and negative.
- Some of us feel overwhelmed, even paralyzed by the violence and tragedy of the world.
- Some of us struggle to overcome what we perceive to be the unfair personal obstacles preventing our happiness and fulfillment.
- Some of us feel trapped by all the negative images, the fear, and the cynicism that we experience on a daily basis.
- Some of us allow all the negativity around us to keep us down and to hold us back from expressing our love to others, our appreciation for ourselves, and our gratitude for life.

At the same time, there are actually some people who don't let all this negativity get to them. Either they've done the internal work necessary to have a genuinely positive outlook on life or they simply choose to be in denial about the bombardment of negativity that exists in our world.

I hope you're getting the picture about how pervasive the attitude of negativity is in our culture. However, I don't share these examples as a way of upsetting you or freaking you out, or to add to all the complaints and blaming that already exist in abundance throughout our culture. I bring this up just to point out that this cultural negativity exists and that we must address and confront these issues effectively if we are going to live a life of appreciation and truly be able to focus on the good stuff. What we see, hear, and engage with on a cultural level—both positive and negative—has a profound impact on us personally.

Questions to Ponder About Cultural Negativity

As we move into Chapter Two and then into the five principles of appreciation, begin paying close attention to all the negative media, the personal blaming, and other dark stuff that you're bombarded with at home and work. Ask yourself how all this negativity affects you personally. The following questions, like the ones earlier in this chapter, are for you to ponder or write answers to, as a way of making the issue of cultural negativity more real and specific for you and your life:

1. What kind of cultural negativity are you most aware of on a daily basis?
2. How negative are the environments in which you live and work? Rate them on a scale of 1 to 10, 10 being the highest level of negativity.

   Home
   Work
   School
   Intimate relationship
   Other

3. During what percentage of your day are you engaging in activities and conversations (looking at information on the Internet, watching the news, reading the paper, listening to the radio, complaining with others) that focus on the negative aspects of our culture and society?

As you consider your answers to these questions, you should be able to see clearly how much impact cultural negativity is having on how you view the world, how you see others, and how you relate to yourself personally. Fully understanding the pervasive nature of this cultural negativity is an essential step in being able to move beyond it so that you can truly focus on the good stuff and live a life of appreciation and gratitude.

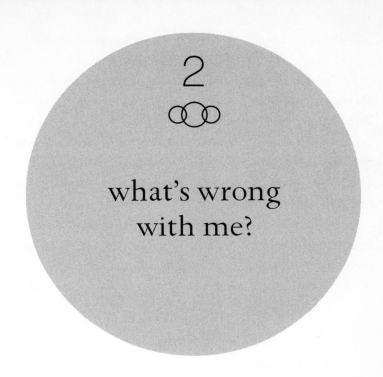

2

what's wrong with me?

Now that we've begun to understand the impact of the negativity we have toward others and the negativity that exists within our society and culture, let's turn our attention to the more personal and damaging negativity that we focus on ourselves: self-criticism.

This is a topic that's difficult for many of us to address, but it's essential to take an honest look at it if we are going to live a life of appreciation and gratitude and be able to focus on the good stuff in a genuine way. The fundamental question here is, What makes it difficult or challenging for us to be grateful for our life, to acknowledge others, and most specifically to appreciate ourselves?

The answer to this question is multilayered, and it varies for each of us. Your answer to this question speaks to your own unique type of personal negativity. For most of us, however, the fact that we are hypercritical of ourselves and that we focus much of our attention on our perceived weaknesses plays a major role in our inability to appreciate ourselves and our lives.

In this chapter, we'll look honestly at this phenomenon of self-criticism—its manifestations in our lives and the negative impact it has on us. Honestly confronting our own self-criticism is what will give us access to true self-love and appreciation.

Negativity Toward Ourselves

Although obviously both the cultural environment in which we live and the way others interact with us have a significant impact on our experience and our level of negativity, we ourselves are in fact the source of all this negativity.

We're each the author of the script of our life. We may want to argue with this, but at some level we all know that it's true. If you've taken the time to pick up this book, wherever you are on your path of personal growth, you know and believe, or at least want to believe, that you create your own reality.

If you take this idea to heart, it's easy to understand that the lack of appreciation and ultimately the intense negativity that we see in the world and that we may express about others is actually a lack of appreciation and negativity toward ourselves.

So let's take a good look at some of the specific ways and reasons how and why we're mean and negative toward ourselves. Fully understanding and dealing with this, just as we did with interpersonal and cultural negativity, gives us an important awareness and framework for our process of creating a life filled with gratitude and appreciation. We must first look at our darkness to see our light.

We're So Hard on Ourselves

Think of some of the negative, critical, and downright cruel thoughts you have about yourself. Most of us would never in a million years say to another human being some of the awful things we say to ourselves about ourselves. If someone talked to us that way, we'd not only dislike that person but possibly argue or even fight with him or her.

In my years as a college and professional baseball player, I learned many things. One of the things I learned to do as well as almost anything else was to beat myself up. I became a master, along with many of my teammates, at being hard on myself and never being satisfied.

These were traits I learned, directly or indirectly, from those around me. I was told that if I was hard enough on myself and never got "complacent," I would be successful in baseball and in life. Guess what? That was a load of bull and I bought it, as do most of us. Many of us are really hard on ourselves, and we obsess about our perceived weaknesses all the time.

The following is a quick and powerful exercise that I often do in my appreciation workshops. If you're willing to be honest and engage with this simple experience, it will give you some insight into how your mind works and where you put your attention.

EXERCISE
Appreciation Assessment

Part 1

Take out a piece of paper or your journal. On the top of the paper write, "Things I need to work on/Problems in my life." Now take a few minutes and honestly list as many things as you can think of that fall into either of these categories. When you're done with this first part, come back to the book to do part 2.

Part 2

Flip the piece of paper over or turn to a new page in your journal. On the top of this sheet write, "Things I'm really good at/Things that are great about me and my life." Now take a few more minutes and honestly list as many things as you can think of that fall into these categories. When you're done with this second part, come back to the book to do part 3.

Part 3

How was this activity for you? Which list was easier for you to make? Which list has more items on it? If you're like the majority of people with whom I work, the first list was actually easier for you to make and may also be longer— assuming you took about the same amount of time to work on each list.

Although there's no right or wrong way to do this exercise, it's usually pretty enlightening and informative for us to take some inventory of the thoughts, feelings, and opinions we have about ourselves and our lives. Remember how this feels and make sure to save your lists. Later in the book we'll do some appreciation exercises, and you'll find it interesting to see if anything has changed for you about how you relate to yourself, your life, and what you appreciate.

Why are we so hard on ourselves, and where did we learn to be this way? Most of us learned it from our parents, siblings, and friends, or from the culture around us. As we discussed in Chapter One, there's a lot of negative and critical energy all around us. In many cases, we had some kind of negative experience as young children and we "learned" to be careful, to make sure we didn't make mistakes, and to criticize ourselves first, before others could do it to us.

The majority of people I meet and work with admit that they are their own worst critics. Being so critical and hard on ourselves makes it very difficult for us to notice all the good things we do every day. This self-critical behavior also gets in the way of our connecting with other people and creating success for ourselves.

For me, self-consciousness about my body and appear-
ance has been a source of great pain, unhappiness, and insecurity at times throughout my life. As a teenager, I grew
ten inches, broke out in horrible acne, and got braces—all
in the same year. I would look in the mirror and see this tall,
lanky, pimple-faced, brace-faced geek.

To this day, there are still times when I look in the
mirror or see a photo of myself and feel like that awkward
fourteen-year-old who feels ugly, goofy, and unlovable. This
is an honest example of how I can be really hard on myself.
In what specific ways are you hard on yourself?

Perfectionism Can Be Dangerous

The term *perfectionist* gets thrown around in a lot of different
contexts. Some of us know that we are perfectionists—for
better or worse. There are many people who are proud and
excited about their perfectionism.

But perfectionism is very dangerous. When we strive
for perfection, we almost always fail, and we set ourselves
and others up for disappointment, stress, and unnecessary
pressure. At some level, we know that each of us is flawed,
that we all make mistakes, and that we often hear or say,
"Nobody's perfect." We may know this, but many of us have
perfectionist tendencies, whether or not we consider ourselves to be an actual perfectionist.

Imagine that in the course of your day you receive a
handful of compliments, along with one piece of critical
feedback. What will you most likely think about and talk

about to others? The critical piece of feedback, right? We get nuts about this.

A great example of this happened to me at the very beginning of my speaking career. In March 2001, I gave my first professional motivational speech. I got hired by Sutter Health on very short notice to deliver a ninety-minute presentation at the end of the full-day management meeting at one of their hospitals. I was excited but very nervous because I needed to create this presentation in less than a week. I'd never given it before, and I would be speaking to a group of 150 hospital managers about whom I knew very little.

When I got to the meeting, my fear shot through the roof. I was twenty-seven years old at the time; the next youngest person in that room was maybe forty. I stood out and felt like a little kid. I could see some skeptical looks in the eyes of many of the people as I came up to the front to deliver my speech. I swear they were thinking, "Who's this youngster, and what does he have to teach us?" As I opened my mouth to deliver the first line of my speech, I was so scared and my heart was beating so loud that I literally couldn't hear anything.

I started with a story, moved into something interactive, and even got a few laughs. All of a sudden, it was going well, and I started to have fun. Before I knew it, the ninety minutes had passed, my speech was done, and I had survived.

A few minutes before it ended, I remember thinking to myself, "I think they're buying this! I wonder if anyone in this room has any idea I've never done this before."

Whether or not they bought it, my speech appeared to be well received. I was really proud of myself for pulling it off. As I was gathering my things, talking to a few people, and receiving some nice compliments from a number of the meeting attendees, a man came up to me and said he wanted to talk to me when I was done.

After the room had just about cleared out, this man told me that he really liked my speech and thought I had done a great job, but wanted to know if he could give me one piece of "feedback."

I said, "Sure, go ahead."

"Mike, you were probably not aware of it, but a number of times throughout your speech, you grabbed your goatee and rubbed it. At first I thought you were doing it on purpose, but you did it so much, I figured it was probably just a nervous habit. It was not a huge deal, but it did start to get a little distracting, so I thought I would let you know."

I listened to what he had to say and thanked him for his honest feedback. In hindsight, maybe I should have said no when he asked me if it was okay to give me some feedback.

Do you know what I thought about the whole ride home from Sacramento, where the meeting took place, to my home in San Francisco? Yep, you guessed it—that guy's feedback. I couldn't stop. I thought to myself, "Those people probably all hated me. They're all driving home in their cars right now thinking to themselves, 'That weird beard-rubbing guy was so annoying; he'll never make it as a motivational speaker doing that.'"

Here I had just given a successful speech, my first ever professional motivational speech, to a large group within a big company and for a good amount of money—by all accounts, a huge win for me—and all I could think about was how I rubbed my beard too much.

If you're a perfectionist and you know it, be kind to yourself, but realize that it's not something to be proud of. If you have some perfectionist tendencies, which most of us do, be very aware of them and notice when they show up; those tendencies can create a great deal of pain, suffering, and self-criticism.

We All Have a Gremlin

Do you remember the movie *Gremlins* that came out in the 1980s? It was about these cute, cuddly little creatures called Mogwais (pronounced Mog Whys), which when fed after midnight turned into nasty green monsters called Gremlins. The Gremlins were able to multiply, create a little army, and terrorize the little town in the movie. Whether you saw the movie or not, you probably have some kind of a visual in your mind of what these Gremlins look like, right?

We all have our own personal Gremlin. You may have heard it called by other names: inner critic, reactive mind, nemesis, saboteur, negative ego, or something else. It is a psychological phenomenon related to the negative and critical thoughts we have about ourselves on a regular basis.

During my coaching training at CTI (the Coaches Training Institute), they used the term "Gremlin" to describe this phenomenon, and it seemed to fit perfectly. I have been talking about the Gremlin in my own work ever since.

Many of us are very familiar with our Gremlin—it is a constant companion for us, and we know its "voice" whenever we hear it in our head. Some of us are not as familiar with our Gremlin; we actually think that its words are our own and that the negative thoughts and ideas coming from our Gremlin are actually true. There are two important points here: first, we must acknowledge that we have a Gremlin; second, it's important for us to create a relationship with our Gremlin so that it no longer runs our life.

If you want to come face-to-face with your Gremlin and hear what it sounds like and thinks like, you can activate it in a very intense way by trying one these:

- Stand up and speak publicly in front of a large group of strange people.
- Take off all your clothes, turn on all the lights, and stand in front of a full-length mirror.
- Take out a photograph of yourself from several years ago and put it right next to a recent one.
- Get up to sing at a karaoke bar by yourself without preparation or rehearsal.
- Next time your boss asks for volunteers, raise your hand before even thinking about what he or she is asking for.

Engaging in any of these activities or even just thinking about doing some of them brings up that Gremlin's voice in your head, doesn't it?

When I first start working with new coaching clients, I always talk to them about their Gremlin and let them know that it will show up in our coaching relationship. For most people, the Gremlin is the one that says, "I can't do that" or "I'm no good at that."

Zack, a former coaching client of mine, was very talented, but was super-hard on himself. Many times in our initial coaching sessions I found myself asking him, "Zack, am I talking to you now or to your Gremlin?" It got so bad that we had to give his Gremlin its own name. To make it easy, we called Zack's Gremlin Jack. All I had to ask was, "Who just said that, Zack or Jack?"

Zack started to see that his Gremlin was getting in the way of his success and happiness. The more Zack started to see how much of his power he was giving away to Jack, the more he was able to see why he'd not been able to create the kind of life he truly wanted.

Most of us give away our power and ultimately our life to our Gremlin. That Gremlin of yours in not interested in your success or happiness; all it is interested in is your survival. One of my early mentors once said to me, "Mike, you're living as though you're trying to survive life. Remember, no one ever does." What a great reminder!

As you read this, I'm sure you can see the negative impact your Gremlin has on your life, your self-esteem, your goals, your success, and your overall sense of self-appreciation. Your Gremlin doesn't want you to appreciate yourself. It relishes your self-criticism, self-sabotage, and demands of perfection.

We Don't Appreciate Ourselves

There are many reasons we have for not appreciating ourselves; this lack shows up in our lives in various subtle ways. When I ask my clients or audiences how good of a job they do genuinely appreciating themselves, I hear a variety of interesting answers. Most people admit they don't do a very good job, or at least they know they could improve. When I ask them why it's hard for them to appreciate themselves, here are some of the most common responses:

- I don't really know how to do it.
- It seems arrogant or like I'm bragging.
- I'm so focused on what needs to get done or what I'm not good at, I don't really notice what is going well.
- I don't want to get lazy or complacent.
- I've never been encouraged to do that.
- It feels uncomfortable.

The most common reasons people have for not appreciating themselves have to do with not wanting to seem arrogant or obnoxious, being uncomfortable, not having the time, or not knowing how.

A simple example of how uncomfortable many of us are with appreciation is how we receive compliments. I see this all the time. So much of the work I do with individuals and groups has to do with appreciation and acknowledgment. It amazes me how awkward many people get when they are genuinely acknowledged by someone else.

The majority of the time when people are given a compliment, especially in public, they do or say something to deflect the expression of appreciation. Listen to what comes out of your mouth after someone compliments you—it's often totally weird or insincere.

These awkward responses take different forms—deflecting the compliment with self-deprecating humor, making a joke that points out some mistake or error, or disagreeing with the acknowledgment in some other way.

For example, a client of mine named Sandy gave a presentation at work, and after she finished, her coworker Frank came up to her and said, "Sandy, that was a great presentation—way to go! I really liked your slides, you made great points, and everyone was engaged."

Sandy replied, "Yeah, well I forgot a bunch of things I was going to say, I talked too fast, and actually skipped over two important slides." Frank then felt uncomfortable about his compliment, and it created an awkward moment for both of them.

The other common thing that people do is throw back an insincere compliment to the person who acknowledged them. They do this even with something simple: Jackie tells Francine that she likes her new hairstyle, and Francine says, "Thanks, Jackie; your new one looks great too," when Jackie hasn't changed her hair in years.

The reality is that with all the negative thoughts going on in our heads, our ridiculous demands of perfection, and our Gremlin in there running the show, it's very difficult for us to hear the positive acknowledgments of other people. Our inability to accept compliments easily and comfortably is a symptom of that. In fact, I bet that the Gallup statistic I mentioned earlier in this chapter (that 65 percent of Americans say they receive no praise or recognition in the workplace) is actually a bit skewed. I'm sure that the numbers and the polling data are accurate, but I'd bet that many of the people surveyed actually do receive praise, but because of their lack of self-appreciation, they aren't able to hear it or let in the acknowledgments that come their way. (In Chapter Seven I talk about how to receive compliments.)

We Project Our Own Negativity onto Others

Another example of our lack of self-appreciation is our negative projections onto others. This relates to our negativity toward other people, but is really a function of our self-criticism. We see negative things in other people because of the way we feel about ourselves.

Projection, a psychological phenomenon that was recognized and explained originally by Sigmund Freud, has to do with our seeing negativity in others that we actually know (or fear) lies within us. According to Freud, "People attribute their own undesirable traits onto others. An individual who unconsciously recognizes his or her aggressive tendencies may then see other people acting in an excessively aggressive way." In other words, we project onto other people the way we, not they, are feeling and behaving.

My coaching client Betty used to talk about her mother all the time, how annoying she was, how controlling she was, and how much she couldn't stand to be around her.

One day I asked her, "Are you like your mother in any way?"

Betty got really upset with me. "I'm nothing like her at all."

She was very angry and self-righteous about it, usually a telltale sign that some projection is going on. At the end of our call, I challenged Betty to think during the next week about her mother and any qualities they shared.

On our next coaching call, Betty said that she hadn't thought about my question for the first few days. She was still pretty annoyed and upset with me for asking it to begin with. The day before our call, however, she noticed herself being really controlling at work, and she stopped dead in her tracks. Betty realized that she was being exactly like her mother in that moment. She ran to the bathroom in tears. As she sat there and cried she realized that all the things she couldn't stand about her mother were actually qualities she shared or was trying to overcome in herself.

We project our negative qualities and tendencies onto others all the time. This covert action is very sneaky and potentially harmful, because most often we aren't aware we're doing it. We're often blind to how we project our own dissatisfaction, disappointments, and weaknesses onto others.

We Don't Honor or Express Our True Emotions

Another of the more complex reasons we tend to be negative toward ourselves (as well as toward others and in general) is that we don't honor or express our true emotions.

We live in a culture that doesn't encourage the passionate expression of many emotions, especially the ones that are considered "bad"—anger, fear, sadness, hurt, shame, guilt. Excitement, joy, love, happiness, and gratitude are okay, but they're often met with cynicism (as we have previously discussed), and even these "good" ones are encouraged to be expressed only in "appropriate" ways and for "appropriate" reasons.

Most of us were scolded in some way, directly or indirectly, for expressing our emotions passionately when we were young, and we've grown up with the idea that being emotionally expressive is a bad thing, can get us into trouble, and is not socially acceptable.

When I was in college, I became deeply depressed. I didn't know what was wrong with me. I'd never felt so awful in my entire life. Every aspect of my life seemed bleak, even though on the outside, my life looked good. I was doing well in school, I was one of the top players on our baseball team at Stanford, I was going to one of the best colleges in the country, I had a girlfriend I really liked, and I had lots of great friends and family members who cared about me. Why was I so miserable?

A few months before, some friends of mine got into a fight on New Year's Eve. I jumped into the middle of the fight in an attempt to break it up. I got punched in the eye and sustained what is known as a blowout fracture to my eye. I couldn't see straight, was struggling with double vision, and was possibly going to require surgery on my eye to correct the problem. All of this happened right before the beginning of my junior season in baseball at Stanford—a very important year for me, as I was hoping to play well and get drafted that June.

The injury freaked me out and set off a chain reaction of negativity within me that knocked me on my ass and led to my depression. I didn't really know what was happening; all I knew was that I didn't want to get out of bed in the morning, and whenever I thought about myself and my life, I felt scared, confused, ashamed, worried, and sad.

I was well aware of depression and its potentially devastating implications. My father was diagnosed with bipolar disorder in his early twenties and had battled with severe depression for most of his life. For my entire life, his depression had been a major source of pain and suffering for him and all of us who knew him. Ultimately, it was his depression that ended his marriage with his first wife and with my mom. Growing up, I was convinced that I would never get depressed. Sadly, I was wrong, and at the age of twenty I was so depressed I thought seriously about ending my own life.

Thankfully, I found a great counselor, Chris, who was able to work with me, teach me things about myself and my life, and introduce me to spiritual concepts and healing techniques that gave me some hope, freedom, and power. He saved my life. It took a number of months of intense sessions with Chris and others before I was able to come out of my depression. My eye injury healed, but more important, my heart and soul healed.

As scary, difficult, and painful as that time in my life was, it was also incredibly enlightening. For me, my depression had more to do with an inability to feel and express my emotions than anything else. Chris helped me realize that I had a great deal of shame, fear, anger, rage, guilt, and sadness within me. It had nothing to do with my eye injury or anything else on the outside; it had to do with the emotions I was denying on the inside and how I felt about myself.

He taught me that these feelings weren't "bad" in and of themselves. It was my inability to acknowledge my real emotions, feel them, and express them that was causing me pain, not the emotions themselves, not my injury, nor any of the other "circumstances" I was mistakenly using as explanations for my depression.

Most recovering drug addicts will tell you that the reason they started and continued to abuse whatever substance they abused was due to some specific emotion or emotions that they feared or were unable to deal with effectively. They will also tell you that even though getting off drugs was the first step in their healing and growth process, it was not in any way the last or most important step. Until they dealt with the underlying issues and emotions that led them to abuse drugs, they could not be free.

Not being aware of our true emotions, not being comfortable with them or not feeling as though we have "permission" to feel and express them, can create debilitating suppression within us. Not knowing how to honor or express our emotions in an effective and productive way is even worse. This dynamic creates a great deal of stress, pressure, and negativity toward ourselves and in general.

The Impact of Self-Criticism

So how does all this self-criticism, suppression of our emotions, and negativity toward ourselves affect our lives and our ability to appreciate? Well . . . it kills off the possibility of our truly loving ourselves, appreciating others, and creating the kind of relationships, success, and happiness that we want.

The negativity we feel toward ourselves, in the various forms we've looked at in this chapter—self-criticism, perfectionism, listening to our Gremlin, not appreciating ourselves, not accepting compliments, projecting our negative attributes onto others, and not honoring or expressing our true emotions—is the ultimate source of all the negativity that we see in others and perceive in the world. Our relationship to ourselves is the source of our lives, and it creates the lens through which we see the world. Whether we see the glass as half empty or half full has to do with how we see and perceive ourselves. How we see and perceive other people is directly related to how we feel about ourselves and our own lives.

Having a deep awareness of the negativity within us is an essential step in our growth and is fundamental to living a life filled with gratitude, acknowledgment of others, and appreciation for ourselves. It takes courage for us to look honestly at this dark side of ourselves. When we are able and willing to do this, we give ourselves the opportunity to confront, heal, and ultimately transform this negativity. In so doing, we can create what we truly want in our world, with the people around us, and within ourselves.

Questions to Ponder About Self-Criticism

As a way of completing both this chapter and the first section of the book, ponder or write answers to these few important questions; your honest inquiry into the impact of self-criticism needs to be as real, specific, and as personal as possible.

1. How does self-criticism show up in your life, and what impact does it have on you and your relationships?
2. What kinds of things does your Gremlin tell you on a regular basis?
3. What specifically stops you from fully appreciating and loving yourself?

As you consider these important questions and your honest answers to them, have compassion for yourself and know that your ability to be authentic with yourself about your own negativity is directly related to your ability to focus on the good stuff and to master the art of appreciating yourself, your life, and those around you. Remember, confronting your negativity and self-criticism honestly is what gives you access to true appreciation.

A Technique to Transform Your Negativity

The following technique will give you a specific and tangible way to confront, address, and transform your negativity.

Feel free to read through it, practice it soon and often, and continue on with the rest of the book. This powerful technique will help you move through your negativity quickly so that you can focus your attention in a more positive and proactive way on what you want and what you're doing. I use this technique myself before speaking engagements, important meetings, family gatherings, and at other times that might create intense negative thoughts or feelings within me. I first learned a variation of this technique from a sports psychologist with whom I worked at Stanford.

Step 1: Acknowledge All Your Negative Thoughts and Feelings Honestly

Think of every doubt, judgment, insecurity, frustration, annoyance, distraction, conflict, and stress that you are having in the moment. The best and most effective way to do this is to speak these thoughts and feelings out loud to another person, someone you trust and feel safe with. The person you're talking to doesn't need to do anything, say anything, or give you any advice. In fact, for this technique to work you want to make sure he or she doesn't do that. The person's job is just to listen to you and hear everything you say, without judgment. Keep talking until you've acknowledged all your negativity, even the stuff you might be embarrassed to say. The more real and honest you are, the more effective this technique will be.

For example, when I'm about to deliver a big speech in front of a lot of people, I might say some things like, "I'm nervous because there are so many people here. I'm scared I will mess up or forget what I want to say. I'm self-conscious about what I'm wearing. I feel ugly. I'm worried I'll sound stupid and people won't like it."

No matter how big or small you think it is, if you're aware of a thought or feeling that seems negative to you, say it. If for some reason you cannot find anyone to listen to you or you're too uncomfortable at first to do this out loud with someone else, there are two other alternatives to step 1. You can speak out loud with no one actually listening—in your bedroom, in your car, or somewhere else. Sometimes if I have to do this by myself in my car, I will just put my cell phone earpiece in my ear so that people in other cars don't think I'm totally nuts. The other option is to write everything down on a piece of paper. Again, this is something I've done a few times if I've been unable to speak to someone or if I'm sitting in a waiting room about to head in for an important meeting and it wouldn't be appropriate for me to talk on my phone or out loud to myself. The key is to get out all your negative thoughts and feelings in a way that works for you.

Step 2: Create a Clean Slate

By acknowledging your negative thoughts and feelings—either by speaking them out loud or writing them down—you'll feel a shift, a "loosening" of the grip of the negativity. This usually happens naturally in your admission of these things. The person working with you, if he or she is good, can help this process by repeating back what you said—just so you know the person heard you and so that you can hear it all again.

My wife, Michelle, does this for me and is great at it. I usually find myself laughing at most of my issues, concerns, fears, and negativity. When you hear it all repeated back to you, it often sounds ridiculous. The goal of this second step is to make sure you've gotten all those negative thoughts and feelings out so that you now have a "clean slate" on which to create.

Step 3: Change Your Physical or Emotional State

Once you've cleared out all the negativity, it's important to change your physical and emotional state. This means that you need to do something physically or say something loudly that will alter your physical and emotional state in some way. If you're able, it's often good to yell, jump, or make a sound or movement that gets your blood pumping and gets you a little fired up. One of my favorites is a nice loud Tarzan yell. That always changes my state in a hurry!

Step 4: Verbalize and Visualize What You Want

Now that you've acknowledged all the negativity, created a clean slate, and changed your state, you're ready to "create" how you want your experience to go. In this step of the process, speak out loud your positive intentions for what you're about to do. In other words, answer the question "How do you want it to go?" Be very specific and make sure to keep each of your statements in the affirmative. For example, don't say, "I don't want to screw it up," or "I hope it's not too bad." Instead, say things like, "I want to feel totally comfortable, alive, and inspired," or "I want them to offer me the job on the spot," or anything positive and specific that you want to have happen. Allow yourself to see and feel it happening exactly how you want it to.

Step 5: Let It All Go

Now that you've gone through the first four steps of this process, it's important to let all of that go, trust yourself, and just be in the moment.

By going though each of these steps, you'll put yourself in the best possible position to truly let it go and know that things will be exactly as they are meant to be. You could've just said that at the beginning, but without actually going through this process and clearing out the negativity, you cannot truly visualize what you want and allow it to happen with ease. This is a process you can now use any time you want to transform your negativity. It's a powerful technique that can have amazing results in your life.

We've looked deeply at both the cultural and personal negativity that gets in our way and makes it difficult for us to focus on the good stuff and appreciate our lives, so we're ready to move into the five principles of appreciation.

part two

the five
principles of
appreciation

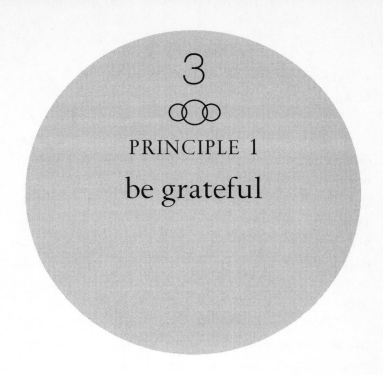

3

PRINCIPLE 1

be grateful

The following chapters present the five principles of appreciation that I teach my clients and that are based on the personal growth work I've done in my own life over the past fifteen years. These principles are designed to give you specific insights, ideas, and techniques that will enable you to live a life of gratitude, appreciation, and fulfillment. The principles are as follows:

1. Be Grateful
2. Choose Positive Thoughts and Feelings
3. Use Positive Words

4. Acknowledge Others
5. Appreciate Yourself

Each principle builds on the one before it; together they create a framework for how appreciation can become a way of life for you and those around you.

The best way for us to transform our negativity and create positive relationships, situations, and circumstances is for us to start exactly where we are and to look at ourselves, others, and the world as they are. Focusing on what we already have and are grateful for right now is one of the most powerful things we can to do alter our life in a positive way.

When I was a child, my mother used to tell me that I "should" be grateful for all that I had because there were other people who were less fortunate than I. Somehow, her saying that never made me feel grateful. Guilty maybe, but not grateful.

Most of us know that gratitude is important. However, we rarely focus much of our attention on what we're grateful for, or we do so because we feel as though we "should," or we remember to be grateful only after something really bad happens.

Being grateful (Principle 1) is fundamental for living a fulfilled life. Gratitude is the first and most basic level of appreciation. It has to do with our outlook and perspective—how we see things and what we're looking for. In this chapter, we'll look at what gratitude is, why it's important, how it shapes our attitude and perspective, and how to have more gratitude in our lives on a daily basis.

What Is Gratitude?

Each of us has our own definition of what gratitude is, and we vary in how we experience it and in how much we focus on it in our daily lives. Most people I talk to and work with admit that they don't focus as much attention as they would like to on being grateful, on feeling gratitude, and on all the good stuff in their lives. According to Dr. Robert Emmons, a psychology professor at UC Davis, coeditor of the anthology *The Psychology of Gratitude,* and one of the world's top experts on gratitude, "Gratitude is one of the most neglected emotions and one of the most underestimated of the virtues."

Many of the reasons for this lack of focus on gratitude were addressed in detail in Chapters One and Two, where we looked at both cultural and personal negativity. Suffice it to say that there isn't a whole lot of encouragement for genuine expressions of gratitude in our day-to-day lives. Therefore, it's important for us to understand gratitude more deeply, and ultimately to be very intentional in our practice of it.

Emotion, Attitude, and State of Being

Gratitude is an emotion, an attitude, and a state of being. We can both *feel* grateful and *be* grateful. Fundamentally, gratitude is a genuine sense of thankfulness and appreciation that we have for someone, something, or for life in general. When we take the time to appreciate someone or something—in thought, word, or deed—we're feeling and often expressing gratitude in that moment.

When we choose to look for the good things in others and find things that we appreciate and are grateful for, we're being grateful—it becomes a state of mind and an attitude. This "attitude of gratitude" is the essence of this principle and is fundamental to our ability to focus on the good stuff and live a life of genuine appreciation and fulfillment.

CHECK THIS OUT
The Physical Impact of Gratitude

According to Rollin McCraty of the HeartMath Research Center and Doc Childre of Quantum Intec, Inc., the expression of genuine gratitude not only keeps social relationships intact but can physically heal our bodies.

In a chapter they published in the anthology *The Psychology of Gratitude*, McCraty and Childre state that cultivating positive emotions, such as appreciation and gratitude, can improve the heart's rhythmic functioning. A well-functioning heart in turn sends signals to the cognitive and emotional centers in the brain.

Why Gratitude Is Important

When we focus on what we're grateful for, we alter not only our perspective but also our state of being. It's almost impossible to feel grateful and victimized at the same time. In fact, feeling and being grateful is a great way to transform our negativity: it can help snap us out of a bad mood, get us back on track, and keep us moving forward in a positive direction. The emotion of gratitude is so powerful that when we feel it, it often overrides any other emotions we're currently experiencing.

In short, gratitude has a miraculous impact on how we see the world. As Oprah Winfrey says, "If you start focusing on what you have and what you're grateful for, you will begin to see more."

A central truth of life is that we always find what we look for, so if we look for things we appreciate and for things we're grateful for, we're likely to find more of this good stuff. Being grateful alters the way we relate to the world and how we see things.

Imagine if you woke up tomorrow morning and made a commitment to be grateful all day long. Even if you held on to that attitude for only the first few hours of the day, do you think it would have an impact on your day, how you felt, and on how you related to others and the world?

Absolutely it would.

Gratitude is a choice. Each day and in every moment we have a choice to feel and be grateful, regardless of our circumstances.

I saw an interview on TV with the actor Michael J. Fox. The interviewer asked him about his battle with Parkinson's disease, how he felt about it, and its impact on his life and career.

Without skipping a beat, Michael said, "I'm grateful for it."

He went on to talk about how much the disease has taught him about himself, others, and life. He also talked about his gratitude for being able to use his name and his resources to increase the public's awareness of the disease and to make a positive difference for those who suffer from it.

What an amazing perspective. Here's a guy who was on top of the world in 1980s and 1990s—the star of two different hit TV shows and many major motion pictures. Now, not only is he mostly unable to act due to his condition, but his life has been significantly altered. Watching him in the interview was not all that easy, as it was clear that on a daily basis he experiences a good amount of physical pain and discomfort.

If he were bitter, depressed, and angry, most of us would understand and wouldn't blame him. Instead, Michael J. Fox has chosen a different approach: one of gratitude, appreciation, and ultimately generosity. This is a great example of the power of gratitude and how we each have a choice to be grateful in our lives, regardless of our situation.

In our daily lives, gratitude not only can help us through challenging times but also can be the catalyst for great change and the source of great happiness. Think of some of the happiest people you know. I bet all of them are people you would consider to be grateful. Grateful people are fun to be around, and they exude a sense of peace, love, and confidence that is often magnetic. I doubt you'll ever hear someone say, "That Nancy—she's just way too grateful."

When I'm working with my coaching clients, I'll often start our sessions by asking them, "What are you grateful for?" However easy or hard it may be for them to answer that question, it always alters their mood, their state of being, and their perspective, and sets a positive foundation for our session.

This also holds true with groups. Before I facilitate a meeting, especially if there's a chance that the group may engage in challenging, difficult, or potentially volatile discussions, I always ask them, "What's going well right now?" It's important for the well-being of the group and the overall success of the discussion that we start in this positive way and talk about some of what people are grateful for, so that we can have a fruitful and effective discussion about issues, challenges, or even goals. Time in and time out, I see this positive approach work, as people open up to the power of gratitude.

Counting Our Blessings

When we take the time to really think about our lives, the people around us, and the world in which we live, there's so much to be thankful for. Think of all the things that had to fall into place and work out just for you to be here in this moment, reading this book.

Depending on your perspective and the specifics of your life story, I would venture to say that there have been literally thousands of miracles in your life that have led you to this specific moment in time.

As Albert Einstein said, "There are two ways to live: you can live as if nothing is a miracle; you can live as if everything is a miracle."

Whether or not you consider yourself someone who has experienced lots of miracles, I'm sure you can admit that many things fall into place every day in your life in a way that works out for you. There are simple things we often consider mundane that we can be grateful for on any given day, such as the touch of another person's hand, a warm smile, the beauty of a tree, that all the stop lights operate properly on our way to work, the food we are able to eat at each meal, and so much more.

EXERCISE
Make a Gratitude List

Take inventory of as many things as you can think of that you're grateful for in your life right now; write them down on a piece of paper or in your journal. You may write down the names of important people, aspects of your life that you like, physical abilities that you have, material possessions that are important to you, important things you've learned, or anything else. You can put anything that comes to mind—big or small—on your gratitude list.

You may want to use the list you created in part 2 of the exercise in Chapter Two as a place to start. Make sure, however, that this is a brand-new list. Take five minutes or more to make your list. Even if you get stuck or feel like you've run out of things, see if you can keep going.

How Gratitude Shapes Our Attitude and Perspective

Dr. Wayne Dyer says, "The way we look at something actually changes what we're looking at." We've all experienced this phenomenon in our own lives. Our attitude or perspective about someone or something has a lot to do with what we ultimately see or experience.

My wife, Michelle, and I used to live in the Presidio in San Francisco. If you've ever been to San Francisco, you may know that the Presidio is a former military base turned national park. It sits on some of the most beautiful real estate in the world—bordering both the San Francisco Bay and the Pacific Ocean. About half a mile from the townhouse where we lived is one of the most breathtaking views I've ever seen—the Golden Gate Bridge, the Marin headlands, and the Pacific Ocean.

We would often walk or drive by that view and say to each other, "Wow—can you believe how lucky we are to live in such a beautiful place?"

Noticing the beauty of that view and acknowledging it to one another always made us feel good, and it reminded us to appreciate it and not take it for granted. Each time we expressed our gratitude for the beauty of the view, it actually seemed to grow more beautiful.

However, there were a number of days when I was in a hurry, running late for a meeting in Marin County, and I needed to drive quickly past the "view point" on my way to

the Golden Gate Bridge. On many of those days and in
many of those moments, not only did I not notice the beautiful view, but I would become annoyed that it existed,
because the number of cars, tourists, and people crowding
around to look were getting in my way and slowing me
down. At those times, everything around me seemed like a
drag. Same beautiful view, different attitude and perspective.

Let's Have Thanksgiving All the Time

On Thanksgiving there's a wonderful tradition in which
many families and groups participate, called "gratitude
sharing." At the dinner table, each person is given an opportunity to share what he or she is thankful for.

I love doing this each year with my family! I always
feel inspired, closer to the people I'm with, and reminded
of the many blessings in my life.

It's wonderful that we take this time to give thanks and
express our appreciation for the good stuff in life. Why
don't we do this more often?

Once again, there seems to be a set of unwritten rules
about public gratitude and appreciation in our society. One
of these rules is that expressions of thankfulness and appreciation should come only at "appropriate" times. Thanksgiving is one of these acceptable times, which is why many
of us take the time and feel at least somewhat comfortable
expressing our gratitude out loud. Birthdays, holidays, wed-
dings, retirement parties, awards banquets, and other similar events or activities also fall into this category. These are

all wonderful occasions for us to express appreciation for ourselves, others, and for life in general.

But what if we did this more often? What if expressing our thankfulness was a regular, everyday occurrence? What if we had "Thanksgiving" all the time? We could—it's up to us.

My friend Johnny recently told me that he, his wife, Lara, and their six-year-old daughter, Isabelle, have "Thankful Thursdays" every week. Each Thursday morning as they're driving Isabelle to school, they all talk about what they're thankful for. Isabelle really loves this activity and looks forward to Thursdays. If Johnny and Lara forget (which some Thursday mornings they do), Isabelle is quick to remind them. She makes sure they take that time in the car to focus on what they're thankful for. This is a perfect example of how we can incorporate gratitude into our daily lives.

Be Grateful for Challenges

One of the most challenging times for many of us to feel and be grateful is when we're facing difficult circumstances in our lives. It seems almost counterintuitive to be grateful for challenges. However, most of us have had really difficult things happen to us, and looking back on some of the most painful challenges, many people (myself included) honestly say that they're grateful to have had those difficult experiences.

For me, my arm injury and the end of my baseball career was one of the most painful and difficult things that had ever happened to me. As I look back on it now, I'm grateful that it happened the way it did. First of all, I learned and grew so much out of that experience. Second of all, had that not happened, I may not have found my deeper passion for personal and spiritual growth, helping people, and doing the work I do now, which I love. Third, if I had continued to play baseball, I never would have met Michelle, the love of my life; we wouldn't be married, and I wouldn't be the proud father of our beautiful daughter, Samantha. These are just a few examples of the many blessings that came out of a very challenging and painful experience for me.

I imagine that you can look back on many of the hardest times in your own life and realize that they "happened for a reason" and that you're grateful now for their going exactly the way they did.

There's a great saying of Carl Jung's that I've heard quoted many times in various workshops and by teachers, coaches, and counselors with whom I have worked: "What you resist persists." In other words, fighting against our struggles and challenges often fails to produce the change that we're looking for. Making peace with our imperfections and even our most difficult challenges will often create enough space to enable us either to make the changes we need to make or simply to be willing to let them go.

As my dear friend and mentor Richard Carlson reminded us in his best-selling book Don't Sweat the Small Stuff, "We fail to recognize that the way we relate to our problems has a lot to do with how quickly and efficiently we solve them."

Our attitude toward a problem we have is usually far more important than the problem itself—in terms of dealing with it effectively or making it into a bigger issue. If we stop and find something to be grateful for in the midst of a challenge, we gain an important perspective that helps us not only "get through" the problem but also learn and grow in the process.

Gratitude Attracts Abundance

When we focus our attention on what we're grateful for, we attract more people, circumstances, and things to be grateful for. Gratitude is one of the greatest forces of attraction in the universe.

My friends Matthew and Terces Engelhart are two of the most inspiring and amazing people I've ever met. They both fully understand the incredible power of gratitude. A few years ago they created a board game and workshop called "The Abounding River." The point of their game and workshop is to teach us to tap into the universal abundance that already surrounds us by being grateful and expressing our gratitude freely.

Many of us think of abundance as having a lot of money or being able to acquire lots of stuff. What Matthew and Terces teach is that we gain access to true abundance by opening up to all that we already have in our lives, being grateful for it, and focusing on what we appreciate about ourselves, others, and life in general.

The Engelharts also opened a café in San Francisco called Café Gratitude. The café was designed to be a living exemplification of their work and their overall philosophy of life.

Café Gratitude is extraordinary. Not only is it beautiful to look at, but it feels good to be there. The food items on the menu are identified by powerful, personal affirmations, such as "I am fulfilled," "I am grateful," or "I am satisfied." You can't just say, "Give me the house salad"; it's the "I am fulfilled" salad.

The café is fun, uplifting, and very positive. It has big tables to accommodate multiple parties. Usually you end up sitting with people you've never met before and striking up very interesting conversations. Cards from the Engelharts' board game are on all the tables, and those cards ask provocative questions, such as "What do you love about your life?" On the bathroom mirror are affirmations—for example, "I love myself," "I am beautiful," or "I celebrate myself." This restaurant is not just somewhere to eat; it's an uplifting experience and a great example of the power and positive impact of gratitude.

Creating More Gratitude in Your Life

With all this talk about being grateful, you may be sitting there asking yourself a very important question: "How do I create more gratitude in my own life?"

This is a great question to ask. The answer is actually pretty simple: practice.

Gratitude, like many other things in life, gets easier the more you practice it. And it literally is a *practice*—a spiritual, emotional, and mental practice. As is true of the other four principles, incorporating gratitude into your life in a significant and powerful way will require your willingness and commitment.

POSITIVE PRACTICES

The great thing about gratitude is that you already know how to feel and be grateful. It's easy, fun, and rewarding. The challenge lies in figuring out how best to remind yourself and to come up with specific practices that you and those around you can participate in regularly.

In this section, I've listed and explained a number of simple gratitude practices that you can use in your life. Most of them can be done alone, but some require other people. All of them are designed to raise your level of gratitude and to launch you in fully practicing this very important principle of *being grateful*.

Some of the practices listed here have already been mentioned in this chapter and book. Some of them you may have done before. And there are clearly many more practices and techniques that you can use. The idea of this list (and of all the positive practices listed in Chapters Four through Seven) is to get you thinking and also to get you into action. My challenge to you is to pick a few of these practices and start doing them today. Have fun, and remember that they're "practices," so you don't have to get them right.

1. Keep a gratitude journal. This is a very simple, powerful practice that can have life-altering results. It was popularized in the late 1990s by Sarah Ban Breathnach in her book *Simple Abundance* and then passionately endorsed by Oprah when she read Ban Breathnach's book and had her as a guest on her show. You can use your gratitude journal any way you like. The goal is to write down five or more things each day that you are grateful for—about yourself, others, or life itself. It doesn't really matter what or when you write—just that you do it and that you commit to doing it every day. Many of my clients find it best to have their gratitude journal right by their bed so that they can write in it when they wake up in the morning or just before they go to bed at night. Some people have told me they like to carry it around with them so that they can write in it throughout the day as they see, feel, and experience things they're grateful for. Make your gratitude journal fun, creative, and unique to you. Ideally have it be something that you like to look at and touch; make it nice and put some of your own style into it.

2. Share your gratitude with others. As mentioned earlier in the section about Thanksgiving, the practice of gratitude sharing can be done at any time with a group of people. Mealtime, especially dinnertime, is a great time to do it. Someone starts and says what he or she is grateful for—from that particular day or in general. When that person's done, everyone else at the table is encouraged to take a few moments to share what he or she is grateful for. Sometimes it helps to give people a specific question: What is something you're grateful for from today? about your job? about your family?

3. Create a morning or evening gratitude ritual. This is another simple and effective practice that you can do alone or with someone else. Sometime in the morning, ideally within the first ten minutes that you're awake, or in the evening right before you go to bed, spend some time focusing on the things you're grateful for. You can use your gratitude journal; talk to your partner, significant other, child, or family member; talk to God in prayer; think about things in your mind; or focus in meditation on what you're grateful for. It doesn't really matter what you do, just so you spend some time and focus some attention on gratitude first thing in the morning or right before you head off to sleep at night. My own morning gratitude ritual often consists of my lying in bed and going through a mental list of things I'm grateful for. I started doing this back in college when I first noticed that it was sometimes hard for me to get out of bed in the morning. Instead of beating myself up for taking some extra time in bed or hitting the snooze button a few times, I decided to make use of that time and focus on gratitude. Similarly in the evening, I will often lie in bed as I'm drifting off to sleep and repeat in my mind some of the many things I'm grateful for—in general or from that day.

4. Ask people what they're grateful for. This practice is very powerful and super-easy. Throughout the course of your day, ask people what they're grateful for. This can be really fun, interesting, and inspiring. It takes a little bit of courage, because some people will laugh at you or think you're weird—believe me, I know! However, most people will love the question and will enjoy answering. Oftentimes they'll ask you in return and then you're able to engage in a wonderfully positive conversation about what you're both grateful for. A fun little twist to this practice is to ask this question on your outgoing voice mail message. For the past few years I've made sure to say some version of "In your message, let me know something that you're grateful for" on all my outgoing voice mail messages—at home, in my office, and on my cell phone. Not everyone who leaves you a message will answer the question, but you'll be amazed at how many people do. Selfishly speaking, I love it because whenever I check my voice mail I get to hear what people are grateful for, which both inspires me and reminds me to think about what I'm grateful for as well. It's also really cool to hear people's reaction to the question—especially those who are calling for the first time or who don't even know me. I've even had people who are calling to sell me stuff leave me messages and tell me things they're grateful for. Pretty neat!

5. Use a gratitude rock. This is a practice that I heard about in *The Secret*, the best-selling book and DVD about the law of attraction. One of the people interviewed in the movie explained this powerful and simple practice. Find a small rock, stone, or crystal that you like. Place it in your pocket or purse and leave it there. Every time you reach your hand into your pocket or purse during the day and touch the rock (which you'll probably do accidentally a number of times), think of something that you're grateful for. At the end of the day when you clean out your pockets or purse, take a moment to think about something (or many things) that you are grateful for. Place the rock on your dresser or counter or wherever you put the things you carry with you each day. The next morning, put the rock back into your pocket or purse and think of something that you're grateful for as you do. And so on. This gratitude rock becomes a symbol and a reminder for you to focus all the time on what you're grateful for.

As you can see, these five gratitude practices are all pretty simple and easy to do. You don't have to do all of them—just pick one or more that resonate with you the most, or create some of your own. Have fun with them. Share them with others. Most of all, make sure you put them into *action*.

Practice, practice, practice. Don't waste your time or energy getting overwhelmed or trying to do these things "perfectly"; just play with them and see which ones fit best for you. The same goes for all the positive practices in this book.

This first principle, Be Grateful, can in and of itself transform your life. When we have an attitude of gratitude, we see what is great in our lives and all there is to be thankful for. Gratitude is an essential piece of focusing on the good stuff and living a life of true appreciation and fulfillment.

Now that we understand the power of gratitude (Principle 1), we can take the next essential step on our journey of mastering the art of appreciating our lives by looking at the importance of choosing positive thoughts and feelings (Principle 2).

4

PRINCIPLE 2

choose positive thoughts and feelings

Being grateful for life as it is right now is the first foundational step in creating a life of appreciation. The second step in this process is to choose our thoughts and feelings and to focus them in a positive direction.

The focus of our thoughts and feelings has a great deal to do with the fulfillment of our relationships, our ability to manifest our goals and dreams, and our overall outlook on life. Our thoughts and feelings are essential aspects of our ability to focus on the good stuff and appreciate our lives.

Principle 2 is not meant to encourage an unrealistic Pollyanna, rose-colored-glasses approach to life. We're talking about consciously choosing our thoughts and our emotions so that we can create the experiences, relationships, and life that we truly want. Choosing positive thoughts and feelings is fundamental to making appreciation and gratitude part of how we live our lives.

The Power of Our Thoughts

Speaker and author Mike Dooley says, "Thoughts become things; choose good ones."

This quotation does a great job of summing up this entire chapter, especially as it relates to our thoughts. For us to live a life of gratitude and appreciation, positive thoughts are fundamental. Creating positive outcomes, relationships, and experiences has a lot to do with the thoughts we think. We've each experienced the power of our thoughts throughout our life.

Positive Thinking
In the summer of 1998, a few months after I got released by the Kansas City Royals, I had a meeting in Menlo Park, California, with a man named Vince Sakowski. Vince, or V-Sak as he's known to those close to him, is about fifteen years older than me. Like me, he played baseball at Stanford, got drafted and played a few years in the minor leagues, and then got released and had to find a "real job."

V-Sak is the unofficial motivator and connector of our Stanford baseball community. In other words, when you're done playing as a former Stanford baseball player—right after college, after a few years in the minors, or even after a decent major league career, you can call on V-Sak and he'll sit you down for a talk.

The reason we all listen to what he has to say is that he's one of the most passionate, positive, and genuinely kind human beings you'll ever find. He also happens to be a phenomenally successful business man and real estate investor.

My meeting with V-Sak that summer of 1998 was incredibly inspiring. He recommended books to me, such as *The Greatest Salesman in the World*, by Og Mandino, and *Learned Optimism*, by Martin Seligman. He also stressed the importance of goal setting, role models, hard work, and focus.

He said, "Mike, you can be, do, and have anything you want. The skills, work ethic, and focus that you learned as a ball player will pay huge dividends for you in life if you use them to your advantage." Then he asked me, "What's your dream? What kind of a life do you want to live?"

I wasn't really sure how to answer that question. He took out a piece of paper and started making a list. He asked me, "Where do you want to live?"

"In the Bay Area," I said.

Then he asked, "Do you want to get married? Have kids?"

"Yes!" I said quickly.

"When do you want to get married, and how many kids do you want to have?" he asked.

"I think I'd like to get married by the time I'm thirty, and I'd like to have two kids," I said.

"What kind of things do you want to do for fun?" he asked.

"Travel, spend time with family, learn, and challenge myself," I said.

"What kind of work do you want to do?" he asked.

I took a while to answer this question. I was a little scared to say it out loud. Finally I said, "I would really love to be writing self-help books, speaking, and inspiring people. However, I'm not exactly sure how to do that at this point, but I can see myself doing that five or so years down the road. Right now, I want to do something fun that makes some good money and teaches me important skills about business and life," I said.

V-Sak proceeded to ask me more questions like this. At the end of his "interview," he'd written down a list of the ingredients for the life I wanted—where I wanted to live, the type of family I wanted to have, the kind of work I was interested in, the amount of money I would need to make to have the lifestyle I wanted, and more. It was fun, a little scary, and very inspiring to talk to him; he was so passionate and excited about what we were talking about. Toward the end of our conversation, he looked at me very intently and held up the piece of paper with my goals and dreams on it.

He said, "Mike, you can have all of these goals and dreams, and even more. You have everything you need—

education, passion, talent, communication skills, support. The only thing that will stop you, get in your way, and make these dreams impossible is your own negative thinking. You've got to keep your thoughts positive. Don't waste your time and energy worrying, doubting, and questioning yourself—that will take you out of the game and keep you from your dreams!"

V-Sak's words and his advice were right on. I'm not sure that I fully realized the wisdom of what he said at the time, but looking back now I can see how insightful he was and how powerful his positive impact was on my life and career, as well as on my own thinking.

Lessons from Norman Vincent Peale and Martin Seligman

Norman Vincent Peale wrote the groundbreaking self-help classic *The Power of Positive Thinking* in 1952, introducing us to many important concepts about the impact our thoughts have on our experience, our emotions, and the overall fulfillment of our life. In the past fifty-five years, many teachers, authors, and even scientists have built on this simple concept of positive thinking.

Monitoring our thoughts and keeping them positive all of the time isn't easy to do, as they seem to come and go very rapidly and somewhat randomly. However, according to Martin Seligman, himself the father and pioneer of positive psychology and author of one of the books V-Sak suggested I read, *Learned Optimism*, there are many things we can do not only to monitor our thoughts but also, more specifically, to become more positive and optimistic in our thinking and outlook. The field of positive psychology has gained a great deal of attention and recognition over the past ten to fifteen years. Positive psychology looks at what's "right" with people, instead of what's "wrong" with them.

Seligman defines optimism as "reacting to life from a perspective of personal power" and pessimism as "reacting to life from a perspective of personal helplessness." Optimism psychology is in the field of cognitive science. It's not magic. According to Seligman, optimism can actually be practiced and learned, even by those who have never considered themselves optimistic in the past.

CHECK THIS OUT
The Impact of Optimism on Physical Health

Martin Seligman and Gregory Buchanan, his colleague at the University of Pennsylvania, conducted a fascinating study with freshmen at the university about the impact of optimism and positive thinking on the health of college students.

In the study, incoming freshmen were asked to complete a questionnaire designed to reflect their overall attitudes and coping behaviors. Seligman and Buchanan invited those students identified as the most pessimistic to participate in the study. Students were randomly assigned either to a sixteen-hour workshop on cognitive coping skills and optimism or to a control group.

Workshop participants learned to dispute their chronic negative thoughts; they also learned positive social and work skills that can help avert depression.

The study showed that the students who participated in the workshop reported fewer physical problems and took a more active role in maintaining their health. In other words, Seligman and Buchanan were able to study and prove that optimism has a significant impact on people's physical well-being.

Positive Expectations

Expectations often have a negative connotation. The word *expectation* itself can stress us out; it's usually associated with pressure we put on ourselves or that others put on us to do, be, or produce something specific. However, positive expectations—of ourselves, others, and life in general—are a valuable tool that we can use to create positive outcomes, results, and relationships.

Expectations are specific types of thoughts that we use to predict the future. Our thoughts have a specific frequency, energy, and impact. There's a great deal of both circumstantial and scientific research that proves that our expectations of ourselves and others play a major role in the outcome of events. When I'm working with clients, I always remind them to increase their expectations because they'll often get exactly what they expect to get—whether it's positive or negative.

Doctors at Wake Forest University Baptist Medical Center conducted a study on the impact of patients' expectations on their perception of pain. The people involved in the experiment were given different levels of heat stimulus, which caused different levels of pain. (None of the levels were high enough to cause burning or to damage to their skin.) The patients were given different expectations by the doctors regarding the amount of pain they would experience. When the doctors gave them positive expectations (that is, told them they wouldn't experience too much pain), there was a 28 percent decrease in the pain ratings that were recorded. This decrease was the same as if the patients had been given a shot of morphine.

"We found that expectations have a surprisingly big effect on pain," said Dr. Tetsuo Koyama, a postdoctoral fellow and lead author of the study.

Expectations have a powerful effect on the outcomes in our life. This Wake Forest Medical Center study and many others like it continue to prove that our thoughts and expectations have an amazing impact on our health and well-being. Further, our expectations of ourselves have a great deal of impact on our ability to achieve our goals, make things happen, and ultimately appreciate ourselves and others. I talk more about the power of positive expectations in Chapter Six.

The Power of Our Feelings

As human beings, we're emotional creatures. Our feelings are fundamental to our experience of life and the circumstances, relationships, and situations we create. Anyone who has ever suffered from clinical depression, as I have, knows the scary and intense power of emotions and the negative impact they can have on his or her life. We must also remember, however, that our emotions can have an incredibly positive effect on our lives. The challenge is that for many of us, our emotions are quite mysterious, changing all the time. We must first confront the power and impact of our emotions and understand their importance; only then can we consciously address our emotions, express them, and more effectively choose the ones we want to feel on a regular basis.

Daniel Goleman, author of the best-selling book *Emotional Intelligence*, says, "Eighty percent of adult success is based upon emotional intelligence." Goleman believes that our emotional intelligence (which he calls EQ) is more important that our IQ. EQ is essentially the awareness of our emotions and the ability to manage them in a healthy and productive manner. Although the concept of EQ has become more accepted in our culture over the past ten years, it's still largely misunderstood and vastly underappreciated.

One common misunderstanding is the notion of "good" and "bad" emotions. Emotions like love, joy, happiness, gratitude, and peace are thought to be good, whereas emotions like hate, anger, sadness, fear, and jealousy are considered bad.

Obviously there are many differences in these emotions, and they have very different impacts on us as human beings. However, it's more accurate and effective to avoid thinking of emotions as good and bad. An emotion is positive when it's appropriately acknowledged and expressed. An emotion becomes negative when it's denied and not expressed.

For example, we've all had positive experiences with some of the so-called bad emotions. Think of the times in your life when your fear came in really handy and saved you from potential harm. Or how about times when you've been really angry at someone, had the courage to express it to the person, and ultimately were able to work out an important issue in your relationship that brought you closer together. In these instances, our "bad" emotions are very useful and important.

We have to be careful in our pursuit of positive thoughts and feelings, and ultimately appreciation, not simply to deny things we consider negative. On the contrary, as we discussed in Chapters One and Two, by acknowledging the negativity that exists around us and (more important) within us, we have the opportunity to transform that negativity into the positive thoughts, feelings, and outcomes we truly want.

The Positive Impact of Our Emotions

Although it's more accurate and effective to think of emotions as positive or negative, depending on whether or not they are appropriately expressed rather than on our standard judgments of good and bad, it's nevertheless important, as I just mentioned, to realize that different emotions have different impacts on us and others. Consider this:

- The emotions we normally consider good (love, peace, joy, passion, appreciation, and so on) usually have a more expansive and creative quality to them. In other words, they bring us closer to ourselves and to each other, and have the ability to help us attract positive results into our lives.
- The emotions we often consider bad (fear, hate, anger, sadness, jealousy, and so on) are usually more restrictive energetically and pull us away from ourselves, others, and our goals.

Another important area that is affected by our emotions is our bodies. There's a great deal of research out there today about the impact of our emotions on our physical well-being. The mind-body connection in medicine used to be seen as "alternative" and is now considered "complementary" if not fundamental to the understanding of health and wellness. Even more than our thoughts, our emotions play a central role in our health and well-being, as well as in our ability to create success, appreciation, and fulfillment in our life.

When we're consciously aware of and in touch with our emotions and able to express them genuinely, we have access to their full power. Developing this emotional awareness and the ability to acknowledge, express, transform, and consciously choose our emotions is a lifelong endeavor. And there are many things we can do to alter our emotional state in a positive direction. Remember, this isn't about ignoring or denying what we're feeling; it's about acknowledging our feelings and choosing to feel a particular way.

Changing Our "State"

When I'm coaching people and they're getting ready to do something important—go out on a first date, make an important presentation, have a crucial conversation with a family member or friend, make a sales call, work on a big goal, or anything else that requires their courage, focus, and positive intention—we talk about "state changes."

A state change is something that you do to alter your emotional and mental state in a positive way. There are many simple ways you can do this; some of which you've probably done throughout your life. Here are some examples of what you can do to change your emotional state:

- Stand up and walk around
- Laugh out loud
- Yell at the top of your lungs
- Engage in physical activity or exercise (run, hike, lift weights, go cycling, play basketball, and so on)
- Listen to uplifting music
- Look at a picture, painting, or photo that makes you happy
- Pray or meditate
- Think of someone or something you love
- Recall a specific positive memory

Any of the activities on this list will change your state and put you in a more positive emotional position to do whatever it is that you have to do. By being in a more positive emotional state, you're more likely to have a positive result.

EXERCISE
Change Your State—Right Now

Before you begin, take a moment to write down your current emotional state. Then do one or more of the things on the preceding list (or something else that you know works for you) to change your emotional state in a positive way.

After you've successfully altered your emotional state, write down what you did specifically and how it made you feel. The goal is to develop a "repertoire" of simple actions that you can take that will change your emotional state quickly and effectively.

The Law of Attraction

Much of what we've been looking at in this chapter related to our thoughts and feelings has to do with the *law of attraction*. Basically, the law of attraction states that things which are alike will be attracted to one another. In other words, we're all magnets attracting experiences, people, and circumstances to us in every moment. If we focus on negative thoughts and feelings, we're going to attract more negative situations and results from other people and life. Similarly, if we focus on positive thoughts and feelings, we'll create positive outcomes. We see this all the time in our daily lives.

For example, think about the last really "bad" day you had. Whether it happened recently or a long time ago, you no doubt remember it well. Most bad days consist of a series of bad things—they seem to build on one another, right? Often we'll think about our bad day, obsess about the circumstances, and even talk about it to others as it's happening, ultimately making it worse. It's as though we have a sign around our neck that says, "I'm having a bad day. Make sure to be rude to me, disappoint me, and give me bad news." This same phenomenon occurs when we have a "good" day. When things are going well, we think positive thoughts, we feel good, and we tend to have lots of good things show up.

Obviously I'm oversimplifying a bit, and it doesn't hold true 100 percent of the time that when we're in a good mood, good things happen, and when we're in a bad mood, bad things happen. However, if you really think about your own and other people's experiences of good days and bad days, it's pretty obvious that we play much more of an active role in the creation of our circumstances than we often admit. In other words, *we create our own reality and attract everything that happens to us.* Most of the good stuff and bad stuff that shows up is a function of our own thoughts and feelings.

Another example of how the law of attraction works is the person in your life who always seems to have some major issue or drama going on—with money, in relationships, with jobs, with her family, and so on. It's usually safe to say and pretty easy to see that this person has something to do with the creation of her dramatic circumstances; after all, she is the common denominator in all her situations. Similarly, you may know someone who seems to be really "lucky" all the time—things just seem to go her way whatever she does. What's actually taking place with lucky people? Whether they're fully aware of it or not, they're attracting all these positive circumstances, relationships, and experiences into their lives based on their thoughts and feelings.

The Law of Attraction in Action

I played baseball at Stanford with a guy named Dan Reed. Dan and I were in the same year at school and were both left-handed pitchers. By our sophomore year, Dan had done so well, he was poised to be the "ace" (top pitcher) of our pitching staff. This drove most of us nuts because he was not the most talented guy on the team. In terms of "stuff" (which for pitchers has to do with speed, movement, and the quality of pitches), Dan was not near the top of the list. His fastball was in the low 80s, his curve ball was pretty good, and his pitches did not seem all that special. How was he able to pitch so well without great stuff? We couldn't figure it out.

Over the course of that sophomore year, the collective jealousy and confusion of our entire pitching staff with regard to Dan's success increased exponentially. Not only was he clearly the ace of our staff, but he ended up winning the conference Pitcher of the Year award, leading us to the Pac-10 conference title and into the NCAA tournament.

In the midst of my own jealousy, I recognized something about Dan that I really respected and admired. First of all, he didn't waste his time and energy worrying about what we thought about him, his talent, or his success. He was pretty focused. Second, he was very confident in his ability. Third, he totally understood the law of attraction.

Dan went out on the mound and expected to be successful, regardless of what the "facts" were about his ability, the speed of his fastball, or anything else. In his mind, he knew he was going to do well and was going to win. He walked, talked, and acted like he had already won, even before the game started. It was not false bravado; it was genuine confidence. Amazingly, he was able not just to win but to succeed at a very high level in the extremely competitive environment of major college baseball. Dan was drafted by the Baltimore Orioles and continued to use the law of attraction to create success for himself in pro baseball. Although arm injuries, inconsistency, and a desire to move on with his life ended Dan's playing career while he was still in the minor leagues, the incredible success he achieved in college was truly remarkable and a clear example of the law of attraction in action.

Positive Visualization

One of the greatest American Olympic athletes of all time was the track-and-field star Edwin Moses. Moses won the gold medal in the 400-meter hurdles at the 1976 and 1984 Olympics. He probably would have won the gold in 1980 as well if the United States hadn't boycotted the Olympics that were held that year in Moscow. Between 1977 and 1987, Moses won 122 consecutive races. Talk about dominance.

I remember watching the 1984 Olympics in Los Angeles on TV and seeing Moses interviewed. When they asked him what made him so successful, he said that in addition to his talent, hard work, and training, he'd learned an important success technique early in his career, and he believed it was what allowed him to perform at such a high level and for so long.

This technique was what he described as "positive visualization." In 1984 this wasn't a common phenomenon the way it is today. Moses explained that he spent a good amount of time during his training and prior to every race visualizing running with ease and winning. He said that he would think about it, see it in his mind, and *feel* it in his body as he visualized.

Hearing Edwin Moses talk in 1984 about the importance of positive visualization was my first introduction to this powerful mental and emotional tool. Since then, I've used positive visualization in sports, in business, and in every area of my life, as well as with many of my clients, to produce amazing results. If you have ever spent any time and energy visualizing what you want, you know that it works with amazing accuracy. And as with anything in else in life, the more you practice the skill of visualization, the easier it gets and the more effective you are in using it.

CHECK THIS OUT
Tips for Visualizing and Creating What You Want

1. Have a clear idea about what you want—write it down or speak it out loud to others.
2. Close your eyes and sit or lie down in a comfortable position.
3. Breathe deeply; relax your mind and body.
4. Think about what you want.
5. See it happening exactly as you want it to happen.
6. Feel the emotions that you associate with being, doing, or having what you want.
7. Hold these thoughts, visions, and feelings for five minutes or more.
8. Open your eyes and "let go" of your attachment to the outcome of your visualization. (In other words, trust that the universe will provide what you want.)
9. Be grateful for what you already have and expect what you want to show up in your life.

Positive visualization is one of the most effective things we can do to use the power of our thoughts and feelings to create exactly what we want in our lives. Practicing and mastering this art is a wonderful way to consciously use the law of attraction to our advantage and to create a life of genuine appreciation.

POSITIVE PRACTICES

The following are a number of simple positive practices that you can use in your life to support you in choosing positive thoughts and feelings.

1. Use the negativity transforming technique. When you're feeling especially negative, use the technique that I explained in detail at the end of Chapter Two in the section "A Technique to Transform Your Negativity." Write down or speak out your negative thoughts and feelings, "clean" them out, and create what you want.

2. Create "vision boards." Vision boards are places that you put text and images describing or symbolizing the goals and dreams that you want to create. Making a collage of positive images that represent what you want to have in your life—love, success, travel, and so on—is a great way to stimulate your thoughts and emotions. Put vision boards up in your office, your bedroom, or anywhere else you spend a lot of time. Look at them, think about them, and get excited when you see them. These boards are a great way to practice the law of attraction and to use your positive thoughts and feelings to manifest what you want.

3. Practice changing your state. Regularly practice putting yourself in the most positive mental and emotional state possible. Use any of the activities mentioned earlier in the chapter, such as listening to uplifting music, laughing out loud, exercising, yelling at the top of your lungs, or simply just standing up. See how effective you can become at putting yourself in a peak emotional state on a regular basis. Being able to do this will enhance your ability to stay positive and attract what you want.

4. Surround yourself with positive images, sounds, and people. As much as possible, surround yourself with positive things and people. Make sure that the images in your physical space, the music you listen to, the radio or television programs you watch, the movies you see, and the people with whom you regularly interact lift you up, make you feel good, and bring positive energy into your life. Although you probably won't be able to create an environment of exclusively positive energy around you, there are many simple things you can do to create more positive images, sounds, and people and to eliminate the negative ones. For example, watch and listen to less news, go to see uplifting movies, and post inspirational quotations in as many places as you can.

5. "Upgrade" your thoughts. Pay attention to your thoughts as much as you can. When you notice a specifically negative thought, whether it is about yourself, someone else, or life in general, see if you can acknowledge it (name it, speak it out loud, or write it down) and replace it with a more positive, empowering thought. As with developing positive expectations, this will take some ongoing practice. Involve others in doing it with you—for support and for fun. Be kind to yourself in the process; don't judge yourself. This practice is all about raising your level of awareness and choosing to focus on positive thoughts.

This second principle of appreciation, Choose Positive Thoughts and Feelings, is fundamental to our ability to live a life of gratitude and fulfillment. Our thoughts and feelings determine how we see the world and experience ourselves and others. By thinking positive thoughts and feeling positive emotions, we set up an internal state within our mind and heart that allows us to see more of what there is to appreciate about ourselves, others, and the world around us. Keeping our thoughts and feelings positive is an essential aspect of our being able to tap into the full power of appreciation.

Now that we've looked deeply at the importance of gratitude and of choosing our thoughts and feelings, we can move on to Principle 3, Use Positive Words, and delve into the power of our speaking. What we say has a lot to do with how much appreciation we have in our lives and how effectively we're able to acknowledge those around us.

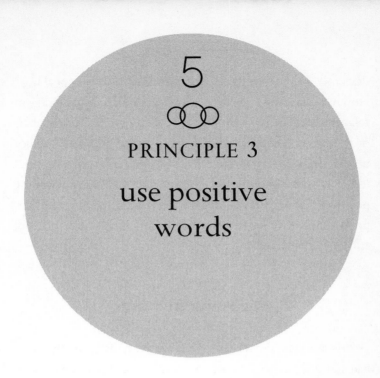

5

PRINCIPLE 3

use positive words

Mother Teresa said, "Kind words can be short and easy to speak, but their echoes are truly endless." I love this quotation and believe in its wisdom so much that I put it on the back of my business card; it also appears on every single page of my Web site.

Principle 3 is Use Positive Words. This principle applies both to how we communicate with others and also to the words we use to describe ourselves, our lives, and the world around us.

Principle 1 focuses on the power of gratitude, and Principle 2 relates to the power of positive thoughts and feelings.

Principle 3 could be titled "the power of positive speaking." How we communicate with others has a huge impact on our relationships with them; and the words we use to describe ourselves, other people, and life in general have a major impact on what shows up in our lives and how we feel about it. This chapter explores some important aspects of speaking positively, how to do it, the impact it has, and why it's important as we strive to live a life of gratitude, appreciation, and fulfillment.

The Power of Words

Words are very powerful. When we were little, many of us learned the phrase, "Sticks and stones may break my bones, but names will never hurt me." Unfortunately this isn't true, and we all know it.

The people who taught us this—our parents, teachers, or friends—meant well in doing so; unfortunately, their wisdom was unfounded. Many of us have been hurt far more by the words of others than by any stick or stone. Sadly, we all know the negative power words can have on us and on our relationships. Each of us has said things that have hurt other people, whether we meant to or not. And how many times has someone said to you, "It's not what you said, but how you said it"?

These examples, though general and somewhat negative, remind us that our words and how we deliver them have a big impact. The good news is that our words also can have an incredibly positive impact. It's important for us to understand the power of our words—as the more conscious and aware we are of our words, the more effective we can be in using them to create appreciation and fulfillment in our lives and with those around us.

CHECK THIS OUT
Our Words Have Power

In don Miguel Ruiz's fantastic book *The Four Agreements*, he teaches four principles designed to give people personal freedom. The first of the agreements is "Be impeccable with your word." In explaining this principle, Ruiz says,

- Speak with integrity.
- Say only what you mean.
- Avoid using the word to speak against yourself or to gossip about others.
- Use the power of your word in the direction of truth and love.

In this agreement and in his book, Ruiz speaks to both the power of words and the importance of speaking positively.

From the book *The Four Agreements* © 1997, don Miguel Ruiz. Reprinted with permission of Amber-Allen Publishing, Inc. P.O. Box 6657, San Rafael, CA 94903. All rights reserved.

Positive Communication

When I am hired by organizations to deliver keynote addresses or seminars, there's one book I almost always refer to in my programs: *How Full Is Your Bucket?* by Donald Clifton and his grandson Tom Rath.

Clifton, who died shortly after completing this book in 2003, was known as the grandfather of positive psychology. He, Martin Seligman, and a few others are responsible for the emergence and prominence of positive psychology over the past ten to fifteen years. Clifton worked for the Gallup organization for almost fifty years and did a great deal of groundbreaking work related to the empowerment and motivation of individuals and groups.

The metaphor in the book *How Full Is Your Bucket?* is simple: we're all buckets of water, and in every single interaction we have with other human beings, we're either filling their buckets with more water or dipping in with a cup and taking water out of their buckets.

This is a bit of an oversimplification, perhaps, but a clear and powerful metaphor nonetheless. Whether we're talking on the phone to a customer service rep, getting a cup of coffee at a café, or having a heart-to-heart conversation with a dear friend, we're either filling the person's bucket or taking water from it, with our words, actions, and attitude. We have to be aware of both sides of our interpersonal interactions. The more aware we are, the more conscious we can become about filling the buckets of other people and noticing who is filling our bucket as well. The book teaches people simple ways to be more positive and to fill people's buckets in a more consistent and effective way. It also uses a great deal of Gallup research to explain how and why speaking positively benefits both individuals and groups.

In *How Full Is Your Bucket?* the authors talk about the "magic ratio" of positive to negative interactions. Experts in the field of positive psychology are finding that the frequency of small, positive interactions is very important. According to the research of John Gottman on marriage, this "magic ratio" of positive to negative is 5 to 1. Gottman claims that marriages are much more likely to succeed when spouses maintain the magic ratio; when it gets down to 1 to 1, there is a high likelihood of divorce.

Gottman and his colleagues conducted a study of seven hundred newly married couples in 1992. They videotaped these newlyweds in a fifteen-minute conversation and counted the number of positive and negative interactions between them. On the basis of his 5-to-1 theory, Gottman and his researchers predicted whether the couple would stay married or get divorced.

They followed up with each couple in 2002, ten years later, to see how things had turned out. Amazingly, they had predicted divorce with 94 percent accuracy. From just a fifteen-minute interaction of newly married couples, Gottman was able to predict the likelihood of divorce with almost perfect accuracy.

The results of this study are a powerful example of the importance of positive communication. There are a number of simple things we can do to be more effective and positive in our communication with others.

Acknowledge Other People's Existence

One of the simplest and most powerful things we can do to create a dynamic of positive communication with someone is simply to acknowledge his or her existence.

Oftentimes this has little to do with anything we might say. People want to be seen, heard, and acknowledged. Being able and willing to pay attention to and acknowledge the existence of others is one of the easiest and most basic ways to support, empower, and appreciate them. Yet it's also one of the most often overlooked.

Our lives today seem terribly busy. So many of us often feel stressed out, as if we don't have the time or the capacity to appreciate and acknowledge the people around us, let alone accomplish our daily tasks and responsibilities.

However, acknowledging other people's existence takes almost no time at all. Looking into someone's eyes, saying hello, asking a friendly question and listening to the response, or stopping what we're doing to give another person our attention are all basic ways we can acknowledge people. We can do these things every day. They take very little effort, but can make a huge difference to the people around us.

A funny but poignant example of the power of acknowledging someone's existence and creating connection happens between perfect strangers all day, every day on freeways around the world. It's what I like to call the "lane merging game."

There you are in your car trying to merge onto the freeway or change lanes in bumper-to-bumper traffic. Sometimes people naturally and in somewhat of an orderly manner take turns merging "zipper style." Often, however, it's not quite that orderly or organized. If you're trying to merge in, you may move your car as close as you can to the spot where you want to be and hope that the person lets you in.

As you know, the best way to make this happen is to get the person's attention and have him look at you; he'll almost always let you in. All it takes is one look from the other driver, and you're golden. If he doesn't look at you, there's a decent chance he won't let you in. On the flip side, if you're on the freeway and someone is trying to merge into your lane and you don't want to let him in, what do you do? You don't look at him, right? You know that as soon as you do look at him, make eye contact, and create a connection—human being to human being—you'll "have to" let him in whether you want to or not.

The key to this example is that when we make a connection and acknowledge someone's existence eye to eye, person to person—even with strangers on the freeway— there's a natural relationship that sparks because in those moments we are usually able to relate and realize that we're more alike than different. That's the power of simply acknowledging someone's existence.

EXERCISE
Acknowledge People's Existence over the Next Few Days

Take a moment right now to think about the next few days and all the potential interactions you'll have. Make a list in your mind or in your journal of the people with whom you'll most likely come into contact. You'll probably interact with friends, family members, coworkers, service people, strangers on the street, people standing in line, and many others. These interactions may be one-on-one, in a group setting, on the phone, or in written correspondence.

Over these next few days, see if you can slow down, be patient, and connect with people in a more genuine and authentic way. Look them in the eye, ask them how they're doing, call them by name, add another line or two to an e-mail where you use their name, ask them a question, or simply wish them a good day and mean it. Acknowledging people's existence is simple and powerful, and it makes a difference.

Listen to People

Listening is one of the most basic but important forms of positive communication and of appreciating and acknowledging other people. Here again, this has nothing to do with our actually speaking, but has everything to do with creating a positive connection with another person and setting up an environment in which positive speaking and communicating can take place. Listening is the key to communication. By listening to people, you let them know that you care, that they're important, and that what they say and who they are matters to you.

How well do you listen to others? How well do others listen to you? For many of us and for a variety of reasons, listening can be challenging. A lot of things get in our way. Usually when we listen, we're not really listening to the other person; we're busy paying attention to the "noise" in our own heads—our opinions, judgments, or even random thoughts that have nothing to do with what's being said. Many of us try to listen and do a number of other things at the same time (in other words, multitasking). And more often than we'd like to admit, perhaps, we're waiting for others to stop talking long enough for us to say what we want to say. All of this keeps us from truly hearing what others are saying and from making any kind of real connection with them. Not listening also creates a fundamental lack of appreciation between us and the other person.

Here's a good example of the power of listening.

Anthony is a manager for a large national construction company. He's responsible for managing groups of construction workers at a variety of job sites. Every day, Anthony runs meetings, gives directions, checks on safety issues, and interacts with his many workers.

One day, after the second of two seminars on positive communication and appreciation I delivered for his company, Anthony stuck around to speak with me one-on-one.

"Mike, those listening exercises we did two weeks ago really worked well for me. Not only have I started using them with my guys in the field, but I've also used them in my personal life.

"My father-in-law, Bill, came over the night after our first seminar, and I decided to practice listening to him. Normally he rarely says much, and when he does, we don't have that much to talk about. However, that night I practiced giving him my full attention, asking him questions, and I became more engaged in what he was saying. At first I felt like I was 'faking it' a little, but after a while it got easier. The more I listened to him and asked him questions, the more he talked. And he definitely started to seem more interesting to me.

"He told me things about his childhood and his time in the military that I'd never heard before. Much of this stuff my wife had never heard either. He even started to ask me questions—something he hardly ever did. We had a great night, and I felt like we connected in a way we've never connected in the eleven years I've known him."

 CHECK THIS OUT
Tips for Effective Listening

- Let people know if you have time to listen to them or not—be honest about it.
- If you miss something that someone says, let the person know and ask him or her to repeat it.

- Be present and fully engaged (don't multitask).
- Let people finish their statements.
- Repeat back or rephrase what people say. (This is not simply parroting; a good rephrase shows people that you have really understood what they said.)
- Engage, ask questions, and make comments.
- Be open to what's being said, even if you disagree.

Stay Positive When Giving Feedback

Many of us are in positions where we have to give other people feedback. For some of us, as parents, bosses, teachers, mentors, or coaches, we give feedback as part of our "job." For others of us, we just like telling other people what we think and giving them "helpful advice." Effective feedback is extremely valuable.

Most of us, however, aren't all that good at giving feedback in a productive and positive way. There are a few main reasons for this. First, we're sometimes too scared to be totally honest with the other person because we think our feedback will hurt his or her feelings. Second, we give feedback to people who don't want our feedback, aren't open to it or ready for it, or haven't given us permission to do so. Third, we give feedback that is either unhelpful or actually damaging. Mostly we do these things unintentionally, but they're debilitating or annoying to others nonetheless.

In my role as a professional coach, one of my main jobs is to give my clients feedback—that is what they pay me for and often why they hire me. Even though I give feedback frequently, it's still challenging and sometimes scary for me. If we want to empower the other person, help him or her out, and create a positive outcome, it's essential that we keep our feedback positive.

Positive does not necessarily mean "nice." However, positive does imply kindness and also that the feedback is solution oriented. Sometimes the nature of the feedback is negative. In other words, the person may have made a major mistake, broken an important rule, or mistaken an important piece of information about which we need to set him or her straight. Whatever the circumstances, we have the ability to "fill people's buckets" even when we give them critical feedback.

Here are some simple steps and reminders you can use to make sure that your feedback is both effective and positive.

1. **Ask permission.** Make sure that you have the person's permission to give her feedback and that she's open to receiving it at that moment. Even if you're her parent, teacher, boss, mentor, coach, or dear friend and the permission may seem "granted," it's important to respect and honor her and make sure she's open to hearing what you have to say.

2. **Acknowledge any fear or hesitation on your part.** If you're nervous or hesitant to give the person feedback, make sure to acknowledge your fear. Doing this is a way to be real and vulnerable; it will take the edge off of the

situation and allow you to relax a bit and connect more with the person—human to human.

3. **Let the person know your positive intention.** Make sure you're clear with him up front about why you're giving him the feedback and what positive outcome you are hoping to achieve.

4. **Let the person know what she's doing well.** Point out what she's doing well and specifically acknowledge her for that. Don't "blow smoke," but make sure to let her know what's going well so that she does not hear the feedback as "all bad."

5. **Use "I" statements.** When giving feedback, make sure to let the other person know that this is only your opinion, not the "truth," and avoid accusing him of anything or even using the word "you" if at all possible.

6. **Let the person know what you want.** Make sure to be very clear about the changes, actions, or specific outcome you would like to see. The more you are clear and positive about what you want to see, the more likely it is that the person will understand what you're saying and the greater the likelihood that a positive outcome will result. If your feedback simply focuses on what the person did wrong and you don't give her any suggestions or make any requests about how to change or improve, she's left without anything positive that she can take away

from your feedback. Make sure to stay solution focused in a positive way.

7. **Acknowledge the person.** Thank him for having the conversation with you, for listening, for being open, and for hearing you and your feedback. Often it takes a lot of courage for someone to hang in and listen to what you have to say, especially if it's critical of him. Thanking him is a great way to fill him up and to ensure that your feedback "lands" in a positive and productive way.

These simple steps and reminders are what I use (in this order) when I'm coaching people, giving feedback, mediating a conflict, leading a seminar on conflict resolution, or addressing an issue or conflict with someone in my personal life. The more volatile the situation, the more challenging it can be to use these steps, but also the more important it is to remember them. The keys to giving effective feedback are honesty and kindness. When we put honesty and kindness up front, we vastly increase the chances that our interactions and conversations will be productive and positive.

Speak Positively About Others

As we discussed in Chapter One, people love to gossip, and gossip can be very damaging to individuals, relationships, and groups. To be someone who speaks positively, appreciates those around you, and lives a life of true gratitude and appreciation, you need to refrain from engaging in gossip.

This isn't easy for most of us to do, because gossip is around us all the time.

One of the companies I've consulted with for the past few years brought me in initially to work with their teams and to address some of the internal conflicts that existed among the team members. After a few meetings with the key players within this organization, it was obvious to me that one of their main issues was gossip. There was a lot of backbiting going on, and a number of the people on each of the teams were not getting along. There were both personal issues between certain coworkers and organizational issues that many people were complaining about.

The process of resolving these issues was not easy—it took a good amount of time, commitment, and courage on the part of all the players involved. However, the resolution process was ultimately simple. Once everyone was able to speak his or her mind, be open and honest, avoid the hearsay and second-guessing of gossip, and really listen to one another, they were able to see that their differences and issues weren't as big as they'd originally believed.

They also were able to see that most of what was both causing and perpetuating the conflicts was their lack of direct communication and the persistence of unproductive gossip. Being able to sit down, create some ground rules and a "safe space," and talk the issues out productively and positively made it fairly easy for them to come to resolution, let things go, and create some new ideas for how to move forward.

❧ A Story of Appreciation ❧

How Leslie Learned to Keep It Positive

Leslie is someone who fully understands the power of positive words and the impact they have on others. She and her husband, Jim, have been together for just under ten years; they have two children and, in her words, "a fabulous, loving, and passionate relationship."

Leslie says, "When Jim and I first got together, I tried to fix him. I would give him lots of helpful advice about how he could do things better in our relationship and in general.

"I noticed that this approach wasn't really working, that he seemed to be getting annoyed and discouraged, and that we were growing apart. Then I learned some new ways to interact with Jim. Instead of telling him what he 'should' do, I started telling him what I wanted—in a genuine and kind way. In addition to letting him know what I wanted, I also made sure to acknowledge him for what he was doing, and I let him know when he did things that made me happy. In a general sense, I made sure to focus on his strengths, what I liked, and what I wanted. If he didn't do what I wanted, I didn't get mad at him about it; I just asked again and continued to acknowledge him in a genuine way."

Jim says, "I love my wife. It's so nice to be with a woman who knows what she wants, asks for it, and takes the time to appreciate and acknowledge me in a heartfelt way. I'm a very lucky man."

Speak About Yourself in a Positive Way

Speaking about ourselves is probably the most important time for us to make sure we're positive with our words. Sadly, our words about ourselves—both in our heads (our thoughts) and the ones that we speak out loud—are often the most negative. As we discussed in Chapter Two, our negativity toward ourselves is one of the biggest obstacles to being happy, fulfilled, and successful. When we speak positively about ourselves and our lives, it has a great impact on our self-esteem, our confidence, and ultimately on what we're able to create in our lives.

In December 2000 I was heading to Dallas for a wedding of one of my former Stanford baseball teammates. Although I was excited that he was getting married and that he'd invited me to the wedding, I was nervous about seeing all my former teammates. It had been about two years since my baseball career ended, and I'd just gotten laid off a few months earlier from my dot-com job.

I knew a lot of people at the wedding would ask me, "What are you up to these days, Mike?" I wasn't sure what I was going to say or how I would feel answering this question.

Jason, my friend who was getting married, was playing pro ball and doing very well, as were a number of my
other former teammates. Many of the guys who'd stopped
playing had high-paying, successful jobs in real estate, fi-
nance, or consulting. I felt like a failure in comparison to
many of these guys.

I was talking to my wife (then new girlfriend),
Michelle, about some of my fears. I said to her, "I'm feeling
really insecure about going down to Dallas and seeing all
the guys. When they ask me what I'm doing, I'm not sure
what I can say besides, 'I'm broke and unemployed.'"

Michelle looked at me very intensely and said, "Don't
say that! Never say that again. Remember the power of your
words. You're not unemployed. Yes, you got laid off a few
months ago and you don't currently have a job. But you
know what you want to do; you're following your heart in
wanting to speak, coach, and write. You have a passion and
a vision that's inspiring. You aren't unemployed; you're
starting your own business."

Her words hit me like a ton of bricks. What she said
was true, but up to that point I had not thought of what
I was doing as following my vision and as actually starting
my own business.

Michelle reminded me about the power of my speaking and challenged me to "upgrade" the words I was using
to describe myself, my work, and my life.

I went to the wedding in Dallas, and although it took
some practice, I did share my vision and my passion for
speaking and coaching, and I told my friends from college

about the business I was starting as a professional speaker and coach. My fear was that they would laugh at me or that I would feel silly talking about it.

To my surprise, the more I talked about it, the more power and confidence I felt. Most of my friends were excited, supportive, and inspired by what I was doing. Looking back on it now, I can see that the conversation with Michelle, my willingness to speak positively about myself and my vision, and the courage I had to share it with my friends, even though I felt scared and insecure at the time, marked a major turning point in my life and a launching pad for my work.

Our words are powerful, and it's essential that we think and choose them consciously, especially when we talk about ourselves. We have the power literally to create our world with the words we speak. Given the choice, doesn't it only make sense that we would want to speak about ourselves and our lives in a positive way? Of course!

POSITIVE PRACTICES

The following is a short list of actions you can take to gain the benefits of positive speaking.

1. Create "gossip-free zones." This is a great practice that you can use at home, at work, or in any other group or environment that you want. A gossip-free zone is a place where you and those around you commit to not gossiping about others. This means that you remind each other, kindly, if someone slips up and starts to gossip. In a gossip-free zone, you and those around you commit to speaking positively about other people. If you have an issue or complaint about someone, you take it directly to that person, get some coaching or feedback from someone else about how to resolve the issue directly, or simply let it go.

2. Go on a "complaint fast." This is a commitment that you make not to complain for a certain amount of time. You may want to start with a day, then move up to a week or even a month if you want to challenge yourself. During this period of time, you commit to not complaining out loud to anyone about anything. It can be challenging, but it's very rewarding. In the process of doing this, you'll train yourself to speak in a positive way and not to waste your precious time and energy on complaints. A great way to do this practice is to get someone else, or even a group of people, to do it with you. Having others involved will create both accountability and support for you.

3. Speak about yourself in a positive way. This is an ongoing, lifelong practice. The first step is to notice the negative things you say about yourself out loud and to stop saying them. You may have to catch and correct yourself a number of times initially. As you do that, the practice is then to see how often you can speak about yourself and your life in a positive way. This isn't about bragging; it's about appreciating yourself and using the power of your words to create the life that you truly want.

4. Communicate your goals and vision in positive language. Write down your biggest goals and dreams in positive language and put them somewhere you can see them every day. If you've already done this, take a look at your goals and make sure that all of them are written in clear, powerful, and positive language. When you speak about your goals and your vision to others, make sure that you talk about them in this same way. Personally, I create a list of personal and professional goals annually. I also have my five-year vision written out, printed up, and posted right above my desk in my office. Many of my coaching clients do the same thing. The most important aspect of creating, writing, and speaking your goals is that you put them in positive language—focusing on exactly what you want.

5. Speak about what you want, not about what you don't want. Pay attention to what you talk about with others. See if you can shift quickly in your conversations from what you *don't* want to what you *do* want. You may be talking about a conflict, a goal, or any random circumstance or situation. Use the power of your words and the law of attraction to focus on and speak about what you want, not about what you don't want. This is another practice that is ongoing and lifelong. It's about becoming more conscious and aware of what you're thinking about and speaking about.

Remember, our words have the power to create, not just to describe.

Principle 3, Use Positive Words, is all about the power of our speaking, the impact our words have on others and our relationships, and how important it is for us to speak about ourselves, our goals, and our lives in a positive way. Now we're ready to move on to Principle 4, Acknowledge Others. We'll take the power of positive words to the next level and focus on how to truly inspire, empower, and thank others with appreciation.

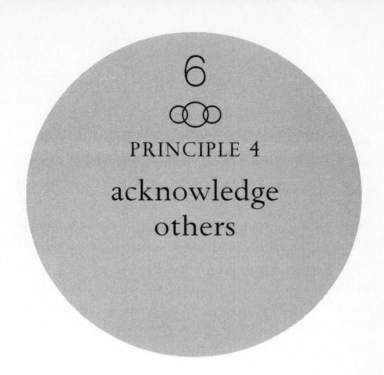

6

PRINCIPLE 4

acknowledge others

Principle 4, Acknowledge Others, takes the first three (Be Grateful, Choose Positive Thoughts and Feelings, and Use Positive Words) and puts them together in a focused way that empowers others, strengthens our relationships, and reminds us of the greatness both within other people and within ourselves.

Acknowledging others is one of the best things we can do to have a positive impact on the people around us as well as to integrate the power of appreciation into our daily lives, our relationships, and into any group with whom we spend our time.

Another great quotation from Mother Teresa is, "There is more hunger for love and appreciation in this world than for bread." People around us are starving for appreciation and acknowledgment, and we have the ability to give them this gift on a regular basis and in a genuine way.

This chapter is all about the art, magic, and power of acknowledging other people. We'll look at why acknowledgment can be hard, the different types of acknowledgment, how to acknowledge people effectively and genuinely, and the positive impact it has on us and others. This principle (Acknowledge Others) and Principle 5 (Appreciate Yourself) are two core elements of all my work and are what I'm usually hired to speak about by groups and organizations. Acknowledging other people and appreciating ourselves are both essential to our living a life filled with gratitude and fulfillment.

Why Acknowledging Others Can Be Difficult

Acknowledgment is an art and a skill that anyone can learn and ultimately master, but many of us have neither taken the time nor had the interest in becoming master appreciators. As the following list shows, there are various reasons why we're not all that good at acknowledging others. The bottom line, however, is that most of us could do a much better job of letting other people know how much we appreciate them and the incredible positive impact they have on our lives.

- We focus most of our attention on what we don't like about people.
- We don't want people to think we're "kissing up" to them.
- They're just "doing their job" or "doing what they're supposed to be doing," so why should we acknowledge them for that?
- Acknowledging others can sometimes feel "cheesy" or awkward.
- We don't know how to acknowledge people in an effective and meaningful way.
- We take other people for granted and don't realize how much we appreciate them until they're gone.
- We're waiting for them to do things *exactly* the way we want them to before we acknowledge them.
- We come from a family, culture, or generation that doesn't acknowledge people openly.
- Acknowledging others is sometimes seen as a sign of weakness or naiveté.
- We're too self-absorbed to notice what other people are doing or their impact on us.
- We're so critical of ourselves, we end up being critical of everyone else.

As you read through this list, you probably noticed a number of examples that fit for you. Which of these "reasons" do you use most often to justify not acknowledging other people? We all have many. Although I respect and appreciate all these reasons and know that for most of us they seem "real," they're all just excuses, and at the end of the day none of them are worth what we miss out on when we don't let people around us know how much we appreciate them.

What Acknowledgment Is Not

One of the main reasons that acknowledging others can be difficult or challenging is that it's often misunderstood or done in a manipulative fashion. Before we can talk about what acknowledgment is and how to do it effectively, we have to talk about what it's not. Acknowledgment is not

- Blowing smoke
- Being "nice"
- Flattery
- Pumping up someone else's ego
- Trying to get something from someone

If your motivation for acknowledging someone is mainly self-interested and you're hoping for a particular outcome from that person, it's not authentic acknowledgment—it's manipulation.

What Acknowledgment Is

Simply put, acknowledgment is any genuine act of appreciation from us toward another person. As we have discussed in previous chapters, looking people in the eye, listening to them, calling them by name, asking them a question, and many other simple actions all fall into the category of acknowledgments. For the purpose of this chapter, we'll focus on acknowledgments in the form of specific acts of gratitude, thanks, and appreciation that we express to other people.

Acknowledgment, like gratitude and other aspects of appreciation, is fundamentally subjective. What we appreciate about other people and what we choose to express to them is up to us and based on our own values, beliefs, and preferences. Although there are a variety of ways we can acknowledge people, there are basically two main types of acknowledgments, reactive and proactive.

Reactive Acknowledgment

Reactive acknowledgment is very common and is what most of us think of when we think of the word *acknowledgment*. Some examples of reactive acknowledgment are

- Recognition for a job well done
- Formal awards
- Results-based monetary bonuses
- Thank-you cards for gifts
- Compliments

Reactive acknowledgment is very important, and it's a crucial aspect of our being able to celebrate, appreciate, and express gratitude for the people around us. For us to integrate the power of appreciation into our daily lives, our relationships, and the groups in which we belong, being good at reactively thanking and acknowledging people is essential.

As the list of examples shows, reactive acknowledgment is always based on something that someone has already done. It's almost always based on performance or behavior, and it often focuses on what people do, not on who they are. Being reactive, it puts all the responsibility on others and leaves us simply to react to them and what they do. Looking only from the perspective of reactive acknowledgment and simply observing another person's results, someone could say, "There's nothing for me to acknowledge about that person because he's not that great, hasn't done anything special, and doesn't really deserve my appreciation," and this statement could be considered true.

Proactive Acknowledgment

The world of proactive acknowledgment is totally different. Proactive acknowledgment puts us as the "appreciator" in a central, responsible place. We're responsible for looking for, finding, and communicating in a proactive way what we like, appreciate, and admire about other people. This means that we do it sometimes for no apparent reason at all and not necessarily for anything that someone has done, and we do it in a creative, passionate, and genuine way.

As we've discussed throughout this book, our focus, attention, thoughts, feelings, and perspective not only determine how we perceive life but also have the ability to attract specific people, situations, and circumstances to us. This means that when we proactively acknowledge specific qualities and actions that we like, want, and admire in other people, we actually bring out and manifest those positive qualities and actions, both in those whom we acknowledge and in life in general. Proactive acknowledgment is very powerful and can be both magical and transformational in our relationships.

CHECK THIS OUT
A Great Quotation About Proactive Acknowledgment

"Remind people who they are instead of just complimenting them on what they've done. Praise and acknowledgment is nice, but that's a bit like telling your dog that his tail wags really well. The idea is to focus on the person behind the accomplishment or problem. It's the fundamental distinction of who versus what. When you help the person get more in touch with who they are, they'll produce better whats. If you focus primarily on the whats, you'll soon be expecting the tail to wag the dog."

—Thomas J. Leonard, *founder of Coach U and CoachVille*
(two of the top coach training organizations in the world)

Another important aspect of proactive acknowledgment is that it's not always connected to results or outcomes. Understanding this comes in handy when we want to acknowledge or appreciate someone who has failed. Although the notion of acknowledging someone when he or she fails may seem counterintuitive to some of us, it's often the most important time for us express our appreciation toward others.

The most effective managers, leaders, coaches, parents, and mentors I know and work with understand this. They know that when someone fails, it's not the time to give the person constructive feedback or to leave him or her alone. When people fail, they often need to be pumped up and supported by us in a positive way. Because they're most likely already being really hard on themselves, the best thing we can do in these moments is to find something in them that we can genuinely acknowledge. Although we may not be able to acknowledge their results, we can almost always acknowledge their effort, and we can definitely acknowledge them as a person.

How to Acknowledge People

We all know how to say thank you, how to give someone a compliment, and how to pat someone on the back to let him know he's done a good job. However, acknowledging others is more of an art than simply going through the motions and actions of appreciation. Although there's no one "right" way to acknowledge people, there are many things we can do and practice that allow us to become more comfortable, powerful, and successful in acknowledging others.

The most important aspect of acknowledging people is our intention. If our intention is to love them, thank them, appreciate them, fill them up, or let them know how grateful we are for who they are, what they have done, and the impact they've had on us, we cannot really mess up our acknowledgment.

The next sections describe the five most important aspects of effectively acknowledging other people:

1. Look for the good stuff and expect it in others.
2. Be genuine and speak from your heart.
3. Thank people in a personal way.
4. Praise people and let them know their positive impact on you.
5. Acknowledge people for no apparent reason.

By remembering and practicing all five of these, you'll be able to touch the hearts of the people you truly want to acknowledge.

Look for the Good Stuff and Expect It in Others

Our expectations have a major impact on other people. For us to appreciate, inspire, and ultimately empower other people, we must have positive expectations of them. When I'm speaking to managers, leaders, teachers, and other people who have jobs in which they lead and influence others, I often say to them, "You'll almost always get exactly what you expect from other people—so expect the best."

Having high expectations of others can be a little tricky. We've all gotten "burned" or hurt by people when we expected something specific from them and they didn't come through. Further, some of us know that our high expectations of others put undue pressure and stress on them and ultimately have a disempowering and negative effect. There's a fine line between having positive expectations that empower people and putting perfectionistic demands on others that they can't achieve and that stress them out.

For us to have a positive impact on other people, we have to work out this balance of expectation and pressure for ourselves and adjust it according to our personality, our relationship with the other person, and the situation. Regardless of the adjustments we must make, it's important for us to understand the importance and impact of our positive expectations on others.

If you expect people to fail, let you down, be jerks, disrespect you, and so on, guess what you'll often find? In contrast, if you expect people to be great, do the right thing, treat you well, get the job done, keep their agreements with you, and be successful, the chances are much better that they will.

One of the first people I ever coached was a woman named Emily. She asked me if I would help her with an important goal she had. Emily was an opera singer, and she wanted to quit her day job in San Francisco, move to Europe, and become a full-time professional opera singer. This was her lifelong dream. Knowing how passionate she was, I had little doubt that she could achieve her goal. In other words, my expectations of Emily were very high; I knew she could make this happen.

Emily told me the steps she needed to take in order to make her dream a reality. She knew exactly what she needed to do; she just had a number of fears and doubts about her ability to make it happen. She didn't think she would be able to raise the money needed for her audition trip. She worried that her German wasn't good enough to communicate with the opera houses. And she was concerned that she wouldn't be able to find places to stay in Europe while she was auditioning.

After less than three months of coaching sessions in which I continued to raise my expectations of and belief in her, Emily had contacted over forty opera houses, set up twelve auditions, raised more than $10,000 for her trip, and found places to stay in each of the cities where she would be traveling to try out.

Two-and-a-half months later, Emily returned and told me she'd been offered a job in Zurich, Switzerland, to be a professional opera singer. She was beside herself with excitement, and I was extremely proud of her.

As Emily's coach, I acknowledged her effort, expected her to succeed, and supported her to stay on track with her goal. Emily's doubt and her Gremlin (that negative voice in her head) tried to take over many times, telling me she couldn't do it and that she wasn't cut out for it, but I didn't buy into that. I kept reminding her of her passion and power—things she knew about herself, but feared. These reminders and my high positive expectations helped motivate Emily to produce these extraordinary results.

Be Genuine and Speak from Your Heart

An essential aspect of acknowledging others is that we must do it in a way that is genuine and real. Phony appreciation and acknowledgment doesn't work and turns people off. We must be real when we thank, compliment, or acknowledge others. The more our appreciation comes from our heart, the more likely it is to have a meaningful impact on the person or people we're acknowledging.

Here are some simple tips to make sure your acknowledgments are genuine:

- **Be specific.** Let her know what you appreciate about her, specifically, or what she did that you want to thank her for.
- **Acknowledge them in person if at all possible.** If you're able to communicate with him face-to-face, it's always the best. Heartfelt e-mails and cards can be effective, but nothing is quite as powerful as an eye-to-eye and heart-to-heart connection. There's a special energy to in-person acknowledgment that cannot be replicated.
- **Look her in the eye and speak directly to her, not about her.** This is especially important if you're acknowledging someone publicly. Don't talk about her in the third person; look right at her, talk to her in the first person, and let the rest of the group just listen.
- **Be spontaneous and present.** When we let the words come to us, rather than plan something specific or read from a piece of paper, what we say is almost always more meaningful and genuine. If you want to think about,

plan, or write down in advance what you want to say, that's okay, but when you actually acknowledge the person, see if you can put that paper aside and just let the words come to you. Trust that whatever there is to say will come out exactly as it should.

- **Say what you mean, and mean what you say.** Simply put, don't blow smoke. Just let him know what you respect, admire, appreciate, or want to thank him for. Let him know how he has affected you in a positive way and why you appreciate him. Keep it simple and heartfelt.

Remember that most of us get nervous when we acknowledge another person in a heartfelt and genuine way. One sign of a real acknowledgment is that one or both of the people exhibit signs of an emotional reaction (nervousness, feeling touched, tears, and so on). This is totally normal and very appropriate. It just means that you're human, that you care, and that you're being vulnerable. These are all good things, even if they're a little uncomfortable. If you experience any of these reactions when acknowledging others, don't worry—it'll pass, you'll live, and the more you do it, the easier it'll get. Just accept that you'll never fully "get over" being nervous; it goes with the territory and is part of being human.

I was delivering a keynote address on appreciation for a government agency at its annual kickoff meeting. The auditorium was full with about 150 people, everyone from this entire department. In the middle of my explanation of the importance of genuineness when acknowledging others, specifically related to public acknowledgment, a woman in the back of the room raised her hand. I stopped and asked, "Do you have a question?"

"No," she said. "I actually wanted to know if it would be okay for me to publicly acknowledge someone right now."

"Sure, that would be wonderful," I said to her. I love it when stuff like this happens when I am speaking or leading a seminar. "What's your name?" I asked.

"Terri," she said.

"Okay, Terri, I have a little coaching for you; is that okay?" I asked.

"Yes," she replied.

"Can you stand up? Ask the person whom you would like to acknowledge to also stand up. Once they do, look them in the eye, speak directly to them, and just let us all eavesdrop on your conversation. Is that cool with you, Terri?"

"Yes," Terri said. "I would like to acknowledge Susan. Susan, can you stand up?"

Susan was the "boss." She was in charge of the entire division, an official appointed by the governor, and a very powerful woman. From the little I knew about Susan and from what I could tell from interacting with her and the group, she was very well respected, but also working at such a high level in the agency that she was probably not able to interact with most of the people in her department on a day-to-day basis, simply due to the nature of her job and the structure of the organization.

I could tell by the reaction of the group that it was a big deal that Terri wanted to acknowledge Susan. And even though we'd already discussed the cynicism that exists with regard to public acknowledgment, especially of the boss or a leader within a group, it seemed as though there was also a reaction to her singling out Susan, and I could see a few folks rolling their eyes in the back of the auditorium.

Susan stood up, and Terri said, "Susan, we've worked together for many years, and although we don't spend a lot of time with one another on a daily basis, I just want you to know that I admire and respect you so much. It's an honor to work for you, and I'm proud to have you as our leader. I'm not sure that many of us take the time to thank you for all that you do and to let you know how much we appreciate you, but I wanted to take this opportunity to do that here, in front of everyone. Thank you."

As Terri's words bounced off the walls of the auditorium, I could sense a certain feeling in the room, the kind of feeling that shows up only when someone is speaking from her heart and expressing true appreciation

There was a pregnant pause after Terri was done. And then, somewhat spontaneously and surprisingly to Susan and the rest of us, Susan burst into tears. When I say "burst," I mean burst: she doubled over and began to sob. It was as if the tears shot out of Susan's eyes like tiny projectiles of moisture. The group gasped loudly, as her outburst took almost everyone by surprise. Terri even shouted out, in a funny and vulnerable way, "Oh no, I'm going to lose my job!" Her comment cut the tension, as it allowed everyone to laugh.

I looked down at Susan, who was still trying to regain her composure. She started to take a few steps and looked as though she were going to leave the room.

"Hold on," I said. "Are you okay?"

I could tell she was fine, just moved and a little embarrassed. I said to the group, "It's okay, she's fine; these are the good kind [of tears]." It was an awesome moment for Terri, Susan, and the rest of us.

 CHECK THIS OUT
The Power of Acknowledgment

Dr. Gerald Graham, dean of the business school at Wichita State University, did extensive research in the mid-1990s on motivation in the workplace and found that employees rated "personal thanks from a manager" as the most motivating incentive of those he studied. This simple interaction was rated more highly than sixty-four other possible incentives, including money, parties, and promotions.

Thank People in a Personal Way

One of my clients, Kyle, recently shared a story with me about the power of thanks. Two of his close friends, Sarah and Jeff, had just moved to Utah from Los Angeles and bought a beautiful new house. Kyle went to visit them for a weekend as their very first houseguest. They had a blast, snowboarding and just hanging out at night cooking dinner and playing cards.

Kyle said that he had the best time of anyone there. Before the weekend, he'd been particularly stressed out and somewhat down about his work situation. He told me that the weekend changed him. Kyle felt rejuvenated, and he came home in a much clearer and more positive state of mind. After his time with his friends in Utah, he was refreshed and eager to make positive changes in his life.

As Kyle reflected on the weekend, he decided to send Sarah and Jeff a handwritten letter instead of an e-mail or a text message. He wanted to let them know how happy he was to see them, how meaningful the weekend was, how much he loved their house, how amazing they were as hosts, and how much he appreciated their support during his challenging time of work transition. Furthermore, he wanted to let them know how much their friendship meant to him in general.

Two weeks later, Sarah and Jeff visited Kyle in Los Angeles. When Kyle saw them, Sarah told him that she had started crying when she read the thank-you letter he'd sent to them. She was deeply touched by his having actually sent them a handwritten note and by his beautiful acknowledgment. She thanked him profusely and told him how much they valued his friendship.

When we thank people in a heartfelt, genuine, and personal way, it can have a huge impact. There are opportunities for us to do this all the time, but we have to look for them, find them, and take action. Both reactively and proactively, there's so much we can thank and recognize about the people around us. The key is that we make sure our acknowledgment is personal.

Praise People and Let Them Know Their Positive Impact on You

My mom used to ask me, "What's the point of thinking something nice about someone if you don't tell them?"

Mary Kay Ash, founder of the Mary Kay cosmetic company, said, "Everyone wants to be appreciated, so if you appreciate someone, don't keep it a secret."

I agree with both of these wise women. Seeing great things in others is totally different than being able and willing to communicate to them how you feel about these great things. Make a positive comment, send a heartfelt note, write an e-mail, leave a voice mail, give a hug, and let people around you know that you appreciate them and specifically what you appreciate about them. This goes beyond thanking people for what they've done; there are people all around you who have not specifically done anything for you, but who are deserving of your praise.

When we praise someone, we look for and find the wonderful qualities about them and let them know. Praise is a step deeper than thanks.

The best way to praise people is to let them know the positive impact they've had on us. Instead of saying, "You're really smart," say, "When I'm around you, I feel more intellectually challenged. Thank you for that." Instead of saying,

"You're fun to be around," say, "When I'm around you I come alive, feel inspired, and have fun. Thanks for having such a great impact on me."

When we let people know the positive impact they have on us, we're sharing our deepest truths with them, and therefore our appreciation has more power. Telling people they are "good" or "smart" is actually just making judgments—positive judgments, but judgments nonetheless. We could just as easily say they're "bad" or "stupid." When we share with people the positive impact they've had on us, we're not simply giving them our judgmental opinion in a positive way; we're telling them who they are in our eyes, what they've done or what quality they have that we appreciate, and, most important, how that positive action or quality has made our life better. This isn't a judgment and it can't be disputed; it's our truth about who they are and the positive impact they have on us.

Signing my professional baseball contract with the Kansas City Royals after my junior year in college was one of the most exciting yet challenging experiences of my life. Although I was fulfilling one of my greatest dreams and goals by becoming a professional baseball player, it was nevertheless hard for me to leave Stanford early.

One of the hardest parts for me was saying good-bye to my pitching coach, Dean Stotz. Dean had been like a father to me. I loved and respected him greatly. He stood by me and supported me through some pretty difficult times in college. He went with me to the doctor's office and stood by my side when it became clear that I needed to have season-ending elbow surgery during my freshman year. He talked to me numerous times during my painful bout with depression. And he constantly supported, encouraged, and championed me—both on and off the field. Although Dean was happy for me and proud of my accomplishments, I knew that he was sad and disappointed that I was leaving school early.

Once I signed my contract and left for my first season in the minor leagues, I sat down and wrote a letter of thanks, praise, and acknowledgment to Dean. I wanted to let him know how grateful I was for his support, his coaching, his mentorship, his guidance, and for the opportunity he and the other coaches had given me to play at Stanford— a dream come true for me. I also wanted to let him know how much I appreciated all that he'd done for me as a person. Dean taught me a lot about being a good man, not just a good baseball player.

Writing that letter felt great, and it was important for me to express to Dean in the note what an incredible impact he'd had on me and my life in my years at Stanford. I dropped the letter in the mailbox in front of the motel where I was staying in Eugene, Oregon (on my first minor league road trip) and didn't think much about it again.

That fall, when I returned home to California, I called Dean to say hello. While we were on the phone, he thanked me for the letter and told me how much it meant to him. He went on to say that in all his years as a coach he'd rarely received thanks and praise from a player the way he had from me.

"You know, people often assume that when you appear to be confident and have a good amount of success, you don't need to be thanked and appreciated. That's not true."

I couldn't believe it. Here was a man who'd been at Stanford for over twenty years; who'd recruited and coached some of college baseball's greatest athletes, such as Mike Mussina, Jack McDowell, and John Elway; and who'd been the architect behind Stanford's back-to-back national championship run in 1987 and 1988. Yet my letter was one of the few heartfelt letters of appreciation he'd received in his career.

A couple of months later, I was at the Stotzes' house for dinner. After dinner and just as I was leaving, Kathy, Dean's wife, pulled me aside and told me what a huge impact my letter had had on Dean. She said that he carried the letter around with him each day in his briefcase as a reminder.

EXERCISE
Acknowledging the People in Your Life

The following exercise is a great way for you to practice appreciating and acknowledging people in your life. This exercise can have a dramatic impact on your relationships and your ability to empower the people around you.

Part 1
On a piece of paper or in your journal, make a list of ten people in your life right now. Next to each name, list at least five things you appreciate about that person and at least one

way he or she has positively impacted your life. When you're done with part 1, come back to the book to do part 2.

Part 2

Read back over your list. None of what you wrote about these ten people is "true." It may be true to you, but it's all subjective—based on your personal opinion and experience of them. This is actually good news, because it means you have the power to appreciate and acknowledge anyone and everyone.

Now add at least two more names to your list. Add some people with whom you interact on a regular basis who you consider to be "difficult" or "challenging." See if you can find five things you appreciate about them and at least one way they've each positively impacted your life. If you really look, you'll be able to find lots of things to appreciate about them. Do this part of the exercise and come back to the book to do part 3.

Part 3

Now for the challenge: in the next seventy-two hours, acknowledge all the people on this list—especially the "difficult" ones. Reach out to them, talk to them in person, pick up the phone and call them, or write them a card or e-mail if you have to. In whatever way you can, get in touch with all these people and let them know what you appreciate about them and how they've positively impacted your life. Do it in a genuine and heartfelt way and see what happens. Have fun!

Acknowledge People for No Apparent Reason

Acknowledging people "for no reason" is the ultimate form of proactive appreciation. I first learned the importance and power of this from my wife, Michelle.

When we first started dating, Michelle sat me down and gave me a long list of things she liked and didn't like. She was very straightforward about it, which I appreciated. It was sort of like a "cheat sheet" for making her happy and a road map for me to navigate in our relationship. I was grateful for the information. One small thing that Michelle mentioned to me in that conversation stuck out. She said, "I really like flowers. But I especially like flowers for no reason."

"What do you mean, no reason?" I asked. To me there were only three reasons to buy flowers for a woman: (1) her birthday, (2) Valentine's Day, and (3) if I did something stupid and needed to apologize. Michelle said, "Buying me flowers for no specific reason at all, just because you're thinking about me, just because you love me, will make me very happy."

A week or so later I saw a flower stand and decided to try this out. Not really sure what her reaction would be, I bought Michelle some flowers for no reason and brought them to her apartment. I gave her the flowers, and she loved it. I mean, she really *loved* it. She got so excited—her face lit up, she smiled, and she actually started jumping up and down. It was wonderful to see her so happy. Because she expressed her appreciation so visibly and so immediately, I found myself searching for flowers wherever I went so that I could bring them to her and make her happy.

I began buying her flowers for no reason all the time. She appreciated the flowers and me so much, and as a result she got more of what she wanted. To this day, I get flowers for Michelle on a regular basis. She "trained" me with her positive reaction, and it ended up being a true win-win.

We don't need to wait for the "right time" or the "appropriate moment" to tell people we love them, what they mean to us, or how much we appreciate them. Sadly, it sometimes takes life smacking us with a figurative two-by-four to the head (a death, accident, or other tragedy) for us to really stop and take inventory of what's important and whom we appreciate. I recently heard someone say, "Don't waste the roses on the casket; give them to the person while they're still alive." I agree with this statement wholeheartedly.

What if we took the time to acknowledge and appreciate the people around us on a regular basis as if it were the last time we were going to see them? What if we randomly created opportunities to let other people know how important they are to us and the positive impact they've had on our lives? We have the ability to do this, and it's really simple. Don't wait until it's too late. Acknowledge the people around you—now. Do it often, from your heart, and for no reason.

Proactively acknowledging people for no specific reason is one of the most generous and positive things we can do for them. And, given the power of our thoughts, feelings, and words, doing this is a wonderful way to manifest and attract great things into our lives, the lives of the people we acknowledge, and our relationships with them. To live a life of appreciation and gratitude and to become a master appreciator, we must have the awareness and ability to acknowledge people in this proactive way.

The Positive Impact of Acknowledgment

At some point in many of my keynotes and seminars, I ask the audience, "Who in your life has impacted you the most?" Audience members raise their hands and respond with the names of parents, teachers, significant others, religious leaders, and friends. Whoever this important person is for each person, there's usually one common theme: it's someone who has appreciated them greatly. Usually, the people who have had the greatest impact our lives are the ones who have believed in our potential and in who we are. They appreciate us and acknowledge us in a way that inspires, motivates, and empowers us to be our best.

Take a moment right now and think of some of the people who've impacted and inspired you the most throughout your life. As you do this, you may find that you want to add a few more names to your acknowledgment list from the exercise earlier in this chapter. When people acknowledge us, it has a real impact. When we acknowledge others, we can literally alter the course of their life.

We all have examples of the positive impact of acknowledgment in our own life. And there are thousands of personal stories and studies that have proven how powerful and important acknowledgment is.

For example, there was a famous study conducted many years ago by Dr. Elizabeth Hurlock, which showed that students who were praised and appreciated for their positive work in school improved their overall performance by 71 percent. Another such example is that according to extensive research done by Gallup, 90 percent of people say that they are more productive when surrounded by positive, appreciative people.

Acknowledgment works. When we're acknowledged, we're more likely to succeed and feel good about ourselves. When we take the time to acknowledge others genuinely, we're able to truly honor and empower them.

POSITIVE PRACTICES

The following is a short list of suggested practices that will enable you to integrate acknowledgment of others into your life on a regular basis.

1. **Write at least one heartfelt thank-you note each week.** At the end of each week, sit down and write at least one heartfelt thank-you note to someone you want to acknowledge. Maybe he did something specific for you that week that you want to thank him for; maybe you've just been thinking about her and you want to let her know; or maybe there's no reason at all, but you want to acknowledge who he is and how he's impacted you in a positive way. Buy a nice box of cards and create a reminder for yourself. In today's electronic, e-mail–

obsessed world, receiving a real, genuine, heartfelt thank-you card, especially out of the clear blue, will have an amazing impact on the person you send it to. Doing this is also a great way for you to practice acknowledging others.

2. **Ask people how they like to be acknowledged.** This is a simple and meaningful practice that works well with friends, family members, significant others, and co-workers (especially if you're a manager or leader). Because the most effective acknowledgment is both genuine and personal, it's important to know how people like to be acknowledged. Everyone's a little different, and acknowledgment is not a one-size-fits-all phenomenon. Simply asking the people around you how they like to be acknowledged is a great way to make sure that when you do acknowledge them, it's meaningful and has the most positive impact.

3. **"Create" the day with your spouse or significant other.** This is a very powerful practice that my wife, Michelle, came up with a few years ago. It's a wonderful example of proactive acknowledgment. This practice is one that you can do with your spouse or significant other each morning. You say to him or her, "Who you are for me today is . . ." and then you "create" your loved one with your words of acknowledgment, such as "loving," "powerful," "beautiful," "wonderful," "fun," and so on. Remember, this practice is all about the creative power of

our words and the magical power of acknowledgment. You want your acknowledgment to be genuine, but it's also important to remember that because of the law of attraction, whatever you focus on, think about, feel, and say has the ability to manifest and create. Michelle and I also add additional pieces to the practice. We also say, "Something I love about you is . . . , "Something I love about your body is . . . ," "Something I love about our relationship is . . . ," and even "Something I love about myself is . . ." And, for the final piece of this practice, we say, "Today I choose you!" Creating the day not only starts your day off in a very positive way but also is an amazing way to connect with and acknowledge your significant other from your heart.

4. **Pick three new things each day that you appreciate about your spouse or significant other and tell him or her.** Pay attention to your significant other and focus on what you appreciate about him or her each day. At the end of the day, sometime in the evening before you go to bed, let your loved one know at least three new things that you appreciate about him or her from that day. The things you chose to acknowledge could be very specific in a reactive way, or they could be more proactive (for example, qualities he or she possesses that you admire). Either way, take the time to let your spouse or significant other know, and create this as a sacred practice of acknowledgment that you do together. It's a great way to complete your day and to appreciate one another.

5. **Put people on the acknowledgment "hot seat."** This is a great exercise that you can do with individuals within a group, team, or family. Each person gets a turn on the hot seat. This hot seat, however, is a positive one, filled with love, appreciation, and acknowledgment. You can put a chair in the middle of the room or you can simply have everyone stay seated where he or she is and just go around the table. When it is someone's turn on the "seat," the rest of the group takes turns acknowledging that person publicly and in a heartfelt, genuine way.

6. **Start off meetings with people sharing "good stuff."** This is a great activity for groups who gather to have regular meetings, especially if those meetings have a tendency to be boring, stressful, or both. Before getting into the agenda of the meeting, it's often nice to open up a short discussion about good stuff. This good stuff could be specific acknowledgments of individuals, announcements of successes, sharing of gratitude for the group in general, or even personal stuff that is totally unrelated (for example, someone talking about their family, a fun trip, or the like). As the person leading the meeting or this short exercise, you can take the lead and either share some good stuff yourself or ask some thought-provoking questions to stimulate the discussion, including

- "What are you grateful for today?"
- "What are some good things that have happened since we last met?"

- "Who has some great news from home that they're excited to share with us?"

This activity takes only a few minutes, but it can make a positive and lasting impression on the group and can help the meeting or gathering be very successful.

Acknowledging other people is fundamental to living a life of appreciation and gratitude. As we become masterful at acknowledging others, we're able to inspire and empower the people around us and create positive environments of appreciation in our lives. Principle 4 is all about our ability to thank, recognize, and appreciate the people in our lives. We're now ready to look at the most important and foundational aspect of all of these principles: appreciating ourselves (Principle 5).

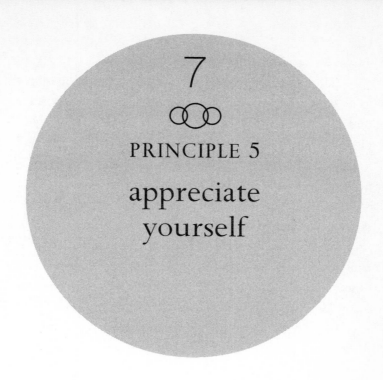

7

PRINCIPLE 5

appreciate yourself

We have now arrived at the fifth and final principle, Appreciate Yourself.

I save this one for last because it's the most important of them all. Not that the first four principles aren't important. They certainly are. Each of them is an essential aspect of living a life of appreciation and fulfillment. However, self-appreciation is the deal breaker. All gratitude and appreciation fundamentally begin and end with our opinion and perception of ourselves. That's why this principle, Appreciate Yourself, is the foundation not only of this book and these principles but of all my work.

Self-appreciation gives us a solid foundation on which to be grateful, focus our thoughts and feelings in a positive direction, use positive words, and acknowledge other people effectively. Without appreciating ourselves, we will find it difficult, if not impossible, to feel, think, and express genuine gratitude about life and toward others.

We live our lives and perceive the world primarily through the lens of our opinion of ourselves—our relationship to ourselves. Whatever we think, feel, and believe to be true about ourselves, so we think, feel, and believe about others and about the world in general—directly or indirectly. How we feel about ourselves is more important than anything else. Underneath everything we do or have ever done is our perception of ourselves and a strong desire to appreciate ourselves. However, we often seem to go about this backwards: trying to succeed, achieve, and prove things to ourselves and others so that we feel deserving of appreciation, instead of appreciating ourselves to begin with.

This chapter looks at why self-appreciation can be very difficult, the difference between appreciating ourselves and being arrogant, some specific things we can do to appreciate ourselves in a genuine and effective way, and why self-appreciation is so important to us and those around us.

Why Self-Appreciation Can Be Difficult

As we discussed in Chapter Two, many of us have a great deal of personal negativity and can be extremely hard on ourselves. We all have that Gremlin in our head that constantly criticizes, judges, and compares us to others in a negative way. Let's take a moment now to address some of the most common reasons why it can be difficult for us to appreciate ourselves.

First, there are many people who don't think self-appreciation is important or who have a philosophical aversion to it in the first place. Second, even those of us who know self-appreciation is important and see the benefit of it in terms of self-esteem, confidence, motivation, and self-care have a very hard time remembering to appreciate ourselves in a way that really has any impact.

Here's a list of some of the most common reasons we have for either not appreciating ourselves at all or not doing it effectively even if we want to:

- We focus most of our attention on what we don't like about ourselves.
- We consider self-appreciation to be egotistical, arrogant, and narcissistic.
- We're embarrassed or feel awkward being self-appreciative.
- We think people will make fun of us or think we're self-absorbed.
- We think that by focusing on our weaknesses we'll improve. (In other words, we're hard on ourselves.)
- We compare ourselves to other people and think that they're better than we are.
- We take our gifts, talents, and successes for granted.

- We're waiting for everything to work out perfectly—then we'll appreciate ourselves and our lives.
- We didn't come from a family or a cultural background where self-appreciation was taught or encouraged.
- We literally don't know how and have never been taught healthy ways to appreciate ourselves.

As you read through this list, you probably noticed a number of examples that fit for you. Which of these "reasons" do you use most often to justify not appreciating yourself? Just as we do with regard to acknowledging others, we all have many justifications for not appreciating ourselves. However, our lack of self-appreciation is often more insidious, and most of us find appreciating ourselves to be even more challenging than acknowledging others. Although I respect, understand, and have compassion for the myriad reasons we all have for not appreciating ourselves, they're all just excuses for us not to do the most important thing we can do as human beings: love ourselves.

Once we understand that self-appreciation is something that is universally challenging, we can have some compassion for ourselves as we work to build our "self-appreciation muscle." As we discussed in Chapter Two, our own negativity and personal struggle with self-appreciation doesn't have to stop us from loving ourselves. In fact, the more we understand our own specific resistance to appreciating ourselves, the more likely we are to move beyond it.

What Self-Appreciation Is Not

One of the main reasons that appreciating ourselves can be difficult or challenging is that it's often misunderstood and misinterpreted. Before we can talk about what self-appreciation is and how to appreciate ourselves effectively, we have to talk about what it's not. Self-appreciation is not

- Arrogance
- An ego trip
- Being better than other people
- Selfish cockiness
- Bragging

The reason many of us feel arrogant, cocky, or self-absorbed when we appreciate ourselves is that we don't draw a clear distinction between bragging and truly appreciating ourselves.

If what we're thinking, feeling, or saying about ourselves in a positive way has anything to do with our feeling superior to someone else, it's not self-appreciation—it's an ego trip. When we're comparing, competing, or thinking we're better than others, we're not appreciating ourselves—we're being arrogant. The differences are subtle but significant. Arrogance is a cover-up for fear and insecurity, whereas genuine self-appreciation is an expression of true love, gratitude, and recognition for something we've done and, more important, for who we are.

What Self-Appreciation Is

Self-appreciation, simply put, is self-love. When we love, value, and acknowledge ourselves for both what we do and who we are, we're appreciating ourselves. It can take a variety of forms, but almost anything we think, feel, do, or say to ourselves or about ourselves in a kind, loving, and positive way fits into the category of self-appreciation.

Here's a list of some simple examples of self-appreciation:

• Celebrating our success
• Speaking about ourselves in a positive way
• Accepting compliments with gratitude and ease
• Forgiving ourselves for mistakes
• Taking care of ourselves—physically, emotionally, mentally, and spiritually

If you look up the word *appreciation* in most dictionaries, it is defined as recognition of the value of someone or something. Working with this simple definition and understanding, we can define self-appreciation as our recognition of our own value. As we're able to see, recognize, and ultimately appreciate in a loving way what we do and who we are, we begin to utilize the true magical power of self-appreciation.

How to Appreciate Yourself

Most of us know how to appreciate ourselves to some degree. Nevertheless, as I've mentioned several times throughout this chapter and earlier in the book, self-appreciation is something that many of us struggle with for a variety of reasons. Not knowing how to do it is often one of the main reasons people have a hard time. Fortunately, though, like acknowledging others, appreciating ourselves is an art, and there is no one "right" way to do it. There are many things we can do and practice that allow us to become more comfortable, powerful, and effective at appreciating and loving ourselves in a meaningful way.

The next sections describe five of the most important aspects of self-appreciation:

1. Accept yourself just as you are.
2. "Be yourself; everyone else is already taken."
3. Focus on your strengths.
4. Celebrate yourself and your success.
5. Acknowledge yourself all the time.

By remembering and practicing all five of these, you'll be able to love and appreciate yourself in a profound and empowering way.

Accept Yourself Just As You Are

My dad always used to say to me, "Mike, you have to accept yourself, warts and all."

I hated it when he said that to me, because even though I knew he was right, there were a number of my "warts" I wanted to change, not accept.

Self-acceptance is an essential aspect of our journey of self-appreciation and fulfillment. We have to begin right where we are. There's a common misconception about acceptance: people often confuse acceptance with surrender or resignation. In reality, however, accepting something doesn't mean that you're resigned about it or that it'll never change.

Acceptance doesn't even mean that you have to agree with something and like how it is. Acceptance simply means that you accept how it is and make peace with it. We sometimes think that if we accept something, we'll no longer want to change it or improve on it; we sometimes consider acceptance as failure.

Paradoxically, the opposite is true. When we fully accept something about ourselves, we then have the space and perspective to look at it and deal with it from a more balanced and healthy place. So much of our suffering as human beings comes from our not accepting things as they are, especially things about ourselves.

Carl Jung's profound truth, "What you resist persists," comes up again here.

You can accept and appreciate yourself and your life, right now. You don't have to wait until you lose the weight, make the money, fall in love, accomplish the goal, or do whatever it is you think you need to do in order to be "good" or "happy." So often we find ourselves waiting for "someday" to appreciate ourselves. We think that after we "make it" we'll be happy and that at that point we'll fully accept and appreciate who we are. As we all know from experience, this kind of thinking doesn't work, and it makes us miserable in the process. The key is to be able to accept and appreciate ourselves in this moment, regardless of what's going on in our lives.

Lisa Earle McLeod, coauthor of *Forget Perfect*, says, "Once you abandon the perfect picture of the way your life *should be*, you can start enjoying the way it *actually is*." This is so true. Too often we listen to the Gremlin's voice in our heads telling us how we *should* be, how we *should* act, how we *should* look, how we *should* feel. Rich Fettke, author of *Extreme Success*, says, "Stop 'should-ing' on yourself."

If you look back at that list of "good" and "bad" aspects of yourself and your life that you made in Chapter Two, you'll notice that most of what's on your "bad" list is stuff that you have not fully accepted about yourself or your life. When we accept ourselves, exactly as we are right now, we create a sense of peace and kindness that allows us to fully appreciate all of who we are.

"Be Yourself; Everyone Else Is Already Taken"

Oscar Wilde, the nineteenth-century author and poet, is famous for his quotations. This one, "Be yourself; everyone else is already taken," is one of my favorites.

We are each unique. We have individual qualities, talents, and gifts that only we possess. Understanding who we are and living true to ourselves are essential to our fulfillment in life. Similar to self-acceptance, personal authenticity is a fundamental aspect of appreciating ourselves. We often get caught up in trying to please others or wanting the approval and acceptance of the people in our lives. Seeking approval can put us on a slippery slope, especially as it relates to appreciation, acknowledgment, and gratitude. Expressing our appreciation for others and having others express their appreciation for us are beautiful things, as long as we remember that our goal in life is not for other people to approve of us and like us. It's much more important that we approve of, like, and ultimately love ourselves—regardless of what others may think, feel, or say. Again, this is somewhat paradoxical, but essential to understand.

When we seek the approval of others and let their opinions of us dictate how we feel and who we think we are—which we've all done in our lives—we give away our power and any real sense of our true selves. The key is for us to be fully ourselves; to own our unique qualities, thoughts, ideas, and feelings; and to express ourselves and live our lives in an authentic way.

As Martha Graham reminds us, "There is a vitality, a life-force, a quickening that is translated through you into action, and because there is only one of you in all of time, this expression is unique, and if you block it, it will never exist through any other medium: and be lost."

Focus on Your Strengths

Many people I know and work with are incredibly talented and accomplished, but you wouldn't know it by talking to them. For example, my friend Edward is a gifted musician and writer, but when I talk to him he constantly downplays his skills and obsesses about his lack of focus, follow-through, and accomplishment. Most of us, like Edward, place far more attention on our perceived weaknesses than we do on our strengths. We either take our strengths for granted or don't value them in a meaningful way.

For us to create the success and fulfillment that we truly want in our lives, we have to be able to know, acknowledge, and utilize all our strengths. To fully appreciate ourselves, and in turn be able to appreciate others, we must acknowledge our own positive qualities.

Another great book that highlights both the ever-expanding field of positive psychology and the extensive research of the Gallup organization is called *Now, Discover Your Strengths*. This groundbreaking best seller, written in 2001 by Donald Clifton (who also coauthored *How Full Is Your Bucket?*) and Marcus Buckingham, along with its "Strengths Finder" assessment tool, have become staples used by leaders, trainers, and organization development consultants in many of the top businesses in the world today. This book and its corresponding assessment tool teach people the importance of discovering and understanding their strengths and also help them ascertain their top five strengths.

Once we discover and own our unique strengths, we're able to understand ourselves better, work more effectively with other people and on projects and problems, and ultimately become more successful and fulfilled in what we do. We also learn that it's more productive, enjoyable, and beneficial to relate to others through their strengths, rather than with a focus on their perceived weaknesses.

My uncle Steve is an amazing man and one of the biggest positive influences in my life. Steve is a very successful psychologist. He told me that for the first part of his career as a psychologist he struggled to find his niche and to be successful. He loved working with people, but didn't love working within the bureaucracy of the agencies he worked for. When he realized that his true strength was in one-on-one counseling, he decided to take a risk and set up a private counseling practice. He followed his passion, pushed through his fears, and focused on his strengths. He said that once he did this, his life and career changed in a dramatic way.

 CHECK THIS OUT
How to Receive Compliments

One of the best ways we can practice appreciating ourselves is to receive compliments from others with gratitude and ease. Do you ever get uncomfortable when someone compliments you? If so, you're not alone. The following are five simple things you can do to improve your ability to receive compliments:

1. Breathe. Make sure to stop and take a nice deep breath when someone acknowledges you.

2. Believe the person complimenting you. Trust that he or she is telling the truth. The more open and trusting you are, the more likely it is that people will give you authentic compliments.

3. Tell your Gremlin to shut up. Don't listen to the negative voice of your Gremlin in your head; instead, listen to the kind words of the person acknowledging you.

4. Don't argue, interrupt, or downplay. Let the person fully acknowledge you and don't deflect the compliment in any way (such as with self-deprecating jokes, disagreement, or minimization).

5. Say thank you and let the compliment in. Just say thanks and then shut up. Whatever you say after thank you is usually phony or some version of deflection. Just breathe and let it in!

Celebrate Yourself and Your Success

Celebrating ourselves and our success is one of the best things we can do to utilize the power of self-appreciation. Here again, we must understand the difference between celebration and bragging. Celebration is about appreciation, satisfaction, and fulfillment. Bragging is about ego, competition, and arrogance. The difference may be subtle, but if we're telling the truth and really paying attention, we'll recognize it.

All too often we take ourselves and our success for granted. It isn't usually until something ends, goes away, or gets threatened that we stop to really appreciate ourselves and what we've accomplished. The fear is that we'll be judged, get cocky, or, even worse, become lazy by celebrating how great we are. Although these fears are understandable, they are unfounded, as true celebration of ourselves and our success will serve only to inspire and empower us.

I work with my coaching clients on this, because for so many of us the concept of celebrating ourselves is foreign.

I'll often challenge my clients to celebrate themselves when they do something, big or small, that they're excited about or proud of. Becoming really good at celebrating yourself and your success takes practice.

Ken, one of my coaching clients, is a writer, editor, and entrepreneur—and like many of us, he struggled with his confidence in his work and with romantic relationships. After we'd been working together for a few months, I gave him an assignment to write down five new things each day that he could celebrate—things he appreciated about himself. Over the course of a month, Ken took part in this daily exercise. He found it difficult and strange at first. However, after a week or so he got into the groove with it and gained a significant amount of insight and self-esteem from his daily self-appreciation and celebration practice.

After the month ended, Ken decided he wanted to continue a version of this exercise in an ongoing way. He said that it helped keep him on a positive track, and he was starting to see some specific results from doing it. Within three-and-a-half months from first starting his regular self-appreciation and celebration exercise, Ken had almost doubled the number of writing projects he was working on. After a long period of social inactivity, he also began dating again—and, more important, he began enjoying himself in these and other pursuits.

Celebrating ourselves and our successes (big or small) allows us to use the law of attraction in a positive way. When we think of celebration in both a proactive way (as cause) and a reactive way (as an after-the-fact phenomenon), we begin to use the power of self-appreciation and the magic of celebration in a way that attracts more positive outcomes and situations to us. Celebration is an essential aspect of self-appreciation and ultimately of our fulfillment in life.

Acknowledge Yourself All the Time

It's essential that we acknowledge ourselves all the time. As we've discussed throughout this chapter and the entire book, there are many different ways to express our appreciation through acknowledgment. The key is our intention, not the specific action. What's important for us to remember with self-acknowledgment is that it must be real, and we have to look for things to acknowledge about ourselves. There are positive things we do, say, think, feel, and achieve all the time. We have so much to acknowledge about ourselves every day, if we're looking for it.

In addition to focusing on our strengths and successes, we can also acknowledge ourselves when we fail. This is often more difficult for us to do, but it is essential. We want to acknowledge ourselves even when we fail so that we train ourselves to accept that failure is okay and that we're okay when we fail. It's not that we want to celebrate the failure, per se, or even that we want to focus on it in a way that will attract more failure; it's that we need to acknowledge ourselves for taking a risk and to take care of ourselves when things don't go how we want them to.

There is usually a success in every failure. Sometimes it's simply that we had the courage to act. Too often our

Gremlin jumps on our failures and uses them against us, both as a way to beat us up and also to give us an excuse not to take risks in the future.

In most of my seminars and keynote speeches, I have people pair up with the person sitting next to them and talk about things they appreciate about themselves. Even if they're paired with a total stranger or they feel awkward initially, most people have a positive and meaningful experience with this simple exercise. We have to train ourselves to focus on and acknowledge the good stuff in our lives and about ourselves. Regularly stop and pat yourself on the back for all that you do and for who you are.

EXERCISE
Appreciating Your Strengths and Successes

Take out your journal or a piece of paper and make a list of all the things you appreciate about yourself. It often helps to split the list up into two categories:

1. Accomplishments and successes (things you're doing or have done)
2. Strengths and qualities (talents and gifts that you possess)

The key is to look for and find as many things as you can to appreciate about yourself. Your Gremlin will probably argue with you about many of these. Don't listen to it. Look deep within yourself and focus on the good stuff. I challenge you to find one hundred or more things to put on this list. Feel free to take as much time as you need, and continue to add to this list through the day or week. You may also want to think about and look for things that on the surface may not fit your picture of what you "should" appreciate about yourself (for example, the courage it took for you to try something, even if you failed).

The Positive Impact of Self-Appreciation

Our deepest fear is not that we are inadequate. Our deepest fear is that we are powerful beyond measure. It is our light, not our darkness, that most frightens us. We ask ourselves, "Who am I to be brilliant, gorgeous, talented and fabulous?"

Actually, who are you not to be? You are a child of God. Your playing small doesn't serve the world. There's nothing enlightened about you shrinking so that other people won't feel insecure around you. We were meant to shine, as children do. We were born to make manifest the glory of God that is within us.

It's not just in some of us; it's in everyone. And, as we let our own light shine, we unconsciously give other people permission to do the same. As we are liberated from our own fear, our presence automatically liberates others.

—*Marianne Williamson*, A Return to Love

This amazing quotation, which is often misattributed to Nelson Mandela, is a great reminder to us of the power, importance, and impact of self-appreciation—both for us and those around us. As Marianne Williamson so eloquently states in this quote, we all have a light and a power within that is both unique and extraordinary. Owning this power is not selfish or arrogant; it's essential for our own growth and for our ability to empower and inspire those around us.

The Many Benefits of Self-Appreciation

The following are some of the many important benefits we receive when we truly appreciate ourselves:

- **Self-confidence.** Appreciating ourselves gives us a genuine sense of who we are, what we have to offer, and our value. Self-appreciation gives us a true sense of confidence and allows us to believe in ourselves.
- **Improved health.** When we appreciate ourselves and our bodies, we're able to improve our health and our overall sense of physical well-being. As mentioned elsewhere in this book, numerous studies have proven that our thoughts and feelings have a significant impact on our health. Having positive thoughts and feelings in the form of self-appreciation is something we can do to enhance our health and create healing in our bodies.
- **A strong foundation for appreciating others.** As we've also discussed elsewhere, we can't honestly appreciate anyone else unless we first appreciate ourselves. Self-appreciation

is the foundation that supports our appreciating and acknowledging others in a genuine and authentic way.

- **Attraction.** Appreciating ourselves is a great way to use the law of attraction in a positive way. When we focus our thoughts, feelings, and actions in an appreciative way toward ourselves, we are naturally going to attract more of the positive qualities, circumstances, and situations that we focus on. Self-appreciation is a great attractor for success and positive outcomes in our lives.

- **Fulfillment.** Our desire for success is mostly based on our deeper desire to appreciate ourselves. When we truly appreciate ourselves, we give ourselves the ultimate gift, and we experience what we're truly after in life: fulfillment. Self-appreciation leads to true fulfillment.

Love Yourself, and Everything Else Will Follow

If we truly love ourselves, most of what we worry about and even much of what we strive for become meaningless. We may still have some worries, and we'll definitely continue to have goals, dreams, and desires. However, when we live our lives from a place of true self-appreciation and true self-love, the fear behind our worries dissipates, and the motivation for our goals dramatically changes: we're no longer driven to avoid or produce things in order to "earn" love; instead, we can focus on our genuine concerns or on something we really want to accomplish.

On the flip side, if we don't fully love and appreciate ourselves, nothing much really matters either. No matter what fears we conquer or what successes we create, we're never able to fully appreciate them or to be fulfilled in the process, because we're constantly striving to be loved.

Self-love is the final puzzle piece of life that we're all searching for. Sadly, we spend most of our lives thinking that someone or something else has that piece. Each of us has our own final piece of self-love within us. To be fulfilled in life, we have to find the love inside and give it to ourselves. There's a hole that only we can fill. No other person, no amount of money, no accomplishment or material possession will do it. It's up to us, and we have an opportunity to appreciate and love ourselves at any time, for any reason.

POSITIVE PRACTICES

The following is a list of suggested practices that will enable you to integrate self-appreciation into your life on a regular basis. Because appreciating ourselves is essential and at the same time quite challenging for many of us, putting some of these practices into action in your life is really important.

1. Create a "sunshine file." A sunshine file, or whatever you choose to call it, is an important folder that you put in your desk drawer (or somewhere else close to you). In this folder, you put any and all expressions of gratitude or appreciation that you receive . . . about *you*. Thank-you notes, cards, photos, awards, and the like can go into this folder. In essence, put in anything that makes you feel good or that reminds you of your own greatness. Keep this folder close at hand and regularly take it out and look through it. This file can also be very helpful when things get tough. Often in the midst of challenging times, we forget to appreciate ourselves. Ironically, it's precisely when things get difficult that it's most important for us to remember the good stuff and to appreciate ourselves.

2. Create regular "me" time. Taking time for yourself is an important way to appreciate yourself. Set up regular "dates" with yourself and do things that you enjoy doing alone. Go on a walk, go to the beach, get a massage, sit and read a book, meditate, or do anything else that makes you feel good. The key is not to "do" too much, but mostly to honor, acknowledge, and appreciate yourself. Your friends, family, and significant other all want you to be happy and to take good care of yourself. This practice is a way for you to do that. It's not selfish. Your taking "me" time will not only benefit you and increase your appreciation for yourself but also benefit those around you because you'll be that much happier.

3. Pick something specific you appreciate about yourself each morning and focus on it all day. At the beginning of each day, pick one specific thing that you appreciate about yourself. It doesn't matter what you choose—a physical quality, an accomplishment, a personal trait, a specific talent, or anything else. The key is to pick something new each day that you genuinely appreciate about yourself and to use it all day to empower you. Throughout the day, if you notice that your Gremlin pops up and has some negative things to say about you, shift your focus away from those negative thoughts and feelings and back to the specific thing you appreciate about yourself. This will help keep you in a positive, self-loving state of mind and state of being.

Picking one specific thing to appreciate will make it easy to remember and focus on when you have negative, self-critical thoughts. By picking something new each day that you appreciate about yourself, you'll continue to build your self-appreciation muscle.

4. Share with a self-appreciation partner. This is a powerful practice that you can do with your spouse, a friend, or anyone you trust. A self-appreciation partner is someone to whom you talk regularly and with whom you can share things that you appreciate about yourself. There's something incredibly meaningful about expressing your appreciation for yourself out loud and having someone else hear it.

Having a specific partner to support us, encourage us, and share with us helps us dig down deep inside and focus on what we appreciate about ourselves. This partnership also helps create the accountability necessary for us to take big actions and make big changes in our lives. Your job is to support your partner in appreciating himself or herself, and your partner's job is to do the same for you. This can be an incredibly magical and empowering relationship for both of you. The most important aspect of this practice, regardless of whom you choose to be your appreciation partner, is that you share what you appreciate about yourself on a regular basis.

Now that we've looked at the reasons why focusing on the good stuff can be challenging (the different types of negativity) and at the five principles essential to living a life of true appreciation and fulfillment, we can turn our attention to the final critical piece of this process: action. It's not what we know, but what we do that really makes a difference in our lives. By living these principles and using the suggested practices, you will become a master of the art of appreciating yourself, your life, and the people around you. The next and final chapter focuses on how to put all this information into action in your life.

part three

∞

appreciation
in action

8

it's not what we know, but what we do that matters

When it comes to creating real growth and lasting change in our lives, it's not what we know, but what we do that matters. Learning new information is fun, exciting, and rewarding. However, until we figure out how to incorporate that information into our daily lives, it does us very little good.

This final chapter is all about how to take what you've learned in this book and put it into action in your life in a meaningful way. I'll recap the key points of the book and talk about the importance of action and accountability. Immediately following this final chapter is a resources section—

a listing of books, workshops, and other sources of information that you can use to further your personal growth and development both in general and as it relates to appreciation and gratitude. The goal of this last chapter is to wrap things up and give you a launching pad for putting appreciation into action in your life.

What *Was* This Book About, Anyway?

Focus on the Good Stuff was set up in two distinct parts. Part One addressed the "problem" that has contributed to the epidemic of negativity in our culture, our relationships, and ourselves. Part Two focused on the "solution": the five principles of appreciation.

Part One: The Problem of Negativity

Negativity on a cultural and personal level is both complex and pervasive. Chapter One looked at the negativity we have toward others and the negativity that exists in the culture around us; Chapter Two looked at the personal negativity we have toward ourselves. The following are the key points of Part One:

- Each of us has challenges and conflicts in our lives, but when we obsess about them, they can keep us under a dark and negative cloud.
- Our negativity toward others (gossip, judgments, and so on) is pervasive.

- There's a great deal of negativity within our culture, and it comes at us from many places (news, media, advertising, politics, conversations).
- Cultural negativity impacts us on a personal level.
- Self-criticism is the most insidious and damaging type of negativity; it's the root of all the other forms.

To fully utilize the power of appreciation in our lives, we have to tell the truth about our own negativity and how it affects our life, our relationships, and our outlook on the world. Part One was designed to delve deeply into our cultural and personal negativity, as well as to describe its impact on us.

Part Two: The Five Principles of Appreciation
The five principles of appreciation described in Part Two are designed to empower you with new ideas, perspectives, and practices for bringing greater appreciation, success, and fulfillment into your life, your relationships, and your communities.

Principle 1: Be Grateful
Start where you are right now; focus on the good stuff in your life and the world in general. When we stop and pay attention to all that we have to be grateful for, we find so much. Gratitude creates success and fulfillment in our lives. Being grateful for all that we have leads us to attract and create more things to be grateful for.

Principle 2: Choose Positive Thoughts and Feelings

Our thoughts and feelings are incredibly powerful. Both what we think and how we feel have the ability to attract positive and negative things into our lives. When we're able to acknowledge and express our thoughts and feelings appropriately, we can consciously choose the positive ones that we want. By focusing our thoughts and feelings in a positive direction, we're able to create a life of appreciation, success, and fulfillment.

Principle 3: Use Positive Words

The words we use—toward others and about ourselves—have great impact. When we use positive words, we're more likely to get what we want, create successful relationships, and feel good about ourselves. Our words have the power to create, not just to describe. Understanding the power of our words and using them in a positive way are both essential aspects of appreciation and acknowledgment.

Principle 4: Acknowledge Others

Expressing our appreciation and gratitude for others through acknowledgment is one of the most loving and empowering things we can do for those around us. Acknowledgment, both reactive and proactive, is the best way for us to connect with people, let them know how much they mean to us, and motivate them in a genuine way.

Principle 5: Appreciate Yourself

Self-appreciation is self-love. Self-love is the most important gift we can give ourselves. If we truly love ourselves, nothing much else matters. If we don't truly love ourselves, nothing much else matters either. When we appreciate ourselves, we make it possible to honestly appreciate others and life in general. Self-appreciation is the foundation for all appreciation.

Appreciation in Action

As this book comes to a close, it's important to ask yourself two very important questions:

1. How does all this information relate to me and my life?
2. What can I do to integrate more appreciation into my daily life?

I hope there have been many times throughout the book when you related personally to the specific examples, points, or exercises. Every chapter has also offered numerous possible practices and actions for you to take. To the degree that you've already engaged in these exercises and practices, all this information is already having a positive impact in your life. As the chapter title states, it's not what we know, but what we do that matters. So what have you done already or what will you do now to put more appreciation into action in your life?

The Power of Action

As a baseball player, I learned that nothing really happened until I got into the game and started playing. The game of baseball takes place on the diamond, not on the sidelines or in the stands. The "game" of your life takes place on the "field" of your real life: in your relationships, at your job, with the people you love, in the day-to-day activities of your life. Reading a book is a wonderful thing to do; it can expand your mind, give you new ideas and insights, and help you tap into new thoughts and feelings that are essential for your growth. However, it's in the application of these new ideas and techniques that your life can transform and where growth really happens.

So often we know exactly what we need to do to make positive changes in our lives. Knowing these things is a good first step, but only if it leads us to take effective action. You can think about and talk about being grateful, acknowledging others, and appreciating yourself, but until you take actions related to these thoughts and words, nothing new happens in your life or in your relationships.

Putting Appreciation into Action in Your Life

Throughout this book there have been many suggestions of possible actions: exercises, a powerful technique for transforming your negativity, and lists of positive practices at the end of each of the chapters in Part Two. Just through reading this book, you've already taken a number of actions that can bring more appreciation, success, and fulfillment into your life.

You've made a gratitude list, a list of things you appreciate about the people in your life, and a list of what you appreciate about yourself. You've practiced changing your physical and emotional state and also thought about ac-knowledging the existence of the people with whom you come into contact on a regular basis. I hope that some of these exercises and actions have already had a positive im-pact on your life, your relationships with others, and how you feel about yourself.

The key is to take some of these actions, or others that you come up with, on a regular basis. Creating regular ap-preciation practices will allow you to enhance your ability to feel, experience, and express your gratitude and appreci-ation in a powerful way.

Go back through the book and your notes and pick out a handful of the exercises, techniques, or practices that were mentioned or that you completed. You can also think of other practices or actions related to appreciation and gratitude—ones that work for your unique personality and style. Put these practices into action in a committed and con-sistent way and watch your life transform!

EXERCISE
Appreciation Practices

What specific appreciation practices will you put into action on a regular basis in your life? Take a moment to think about and write down what actions or practices you'll take in your life on a regular basis as a result of reading this book.

You can use your journal, a piece of paper, or the space below to write these down. The key is to pick a handful of

actions that suit you, write them down, and let other people
know about them. Doing this will increase the likelihood of
your success and allow you to put appreciation effectively
into action in your life.

_____

_____

_____

_____

_____

_____

Accountability

One of the best ways you can support yourself in taking on
these new practices and in making positive changes in your
life in general is to create accountability for yourself. Most
of us resist accountability because we don't want to add any
extra pressure to our already busy lives. We've also all had
experiences in the past where we failed, let someone down,
or had a negative experience with accountability.

However, accountability can be magical. It's such a
great support and motivator for us when we want to make
positive changes or reach new heights. Most of my job as a
personal coach is to hold my clients accountable so that
they take positive actions toward their most important goals
and dreams. By making regular commitments about what
they'll do and what they want to manifest in their lives, my

clients are able to produce breakthrough results and expand themselves in ways they didn't think they could.

In my own life, I've had some amazing coaches, mentors, and success partners who've all played a vital role in my own success and growth. They've supported me and pushed me by holding me accountable. Without accountability, many of our good ideas and intentions remain just ideas and intentions. With accountability, we're able to put them into action.

Think about ways you can create more effective accountability in your own life. Hire a professional coach, elicit the support of mentors, create a "mastermind" support group of like-minded and success-oriented peers, ask a friend to be your accountability buddy and share goals and commitments with her, or do anything else that you know will create the support and accountability you need.

Choice and Commitment

Fundamentally, focusing on the good stuff comes down to choice and commitment. What kind of life do you want? How do you want to look at the world, treat others, and relate to yourself? Given that you picked up this book and have read all the way through to this point, I assume that living a life of appreciation and gratitude can help you with the unique circumstances of your life. More important, I know that you now know (and probably did even before reading this book) that appreciation is the most important aspect of creating the kind of fulfilling life you truly want.

I acknowledge you for your interest in and commitment to appreciating yourself, others, and your life. Making greater appreciation and gratitude a reality in your daily life will take a strong commitment on your part. It's not a commitment to be perfect or to be always positive; those are unrealistic expectations of yourself. Your commitment needs to be to staying conscious—to being aware of your environment, your thoughts, your feelings, your words, and your deeds. This commitment and a willingness to take actions that will lead you toward greater peace, appreciation, and fulfillment—with others and with yourself—are what will enable you to become a true master at the art of appreciating yourself, your life, and those around you!

A Final Word of
Acknowledgment for You

From the bottom of my heart, I thank you for reading this book. I'm honored and grateful to have been able to connect with you in this way, and it means so much to me to be able to share my work. I hope you enjoyed this book and were able to take away some meaningful insights and actions.

Specifically, I want to acknowledge you for your commitment to your own growth, for engaging in this material and these exercises, and for being someone who is committed to loving yourself, others, and the world in which you live. I look forward to having an opportunity to work with you again in the future. I also would love to hear how you're doing as you travel on your path of appreciation and gratitude.

Please let me know how things are going by writing to me at my e-mail address, given below. And remember, don't wait until it's too late: appreciate yourself, others, and life right now!

With gratitude and appreciation,
Mike Robbins
mike@mike-robbins.com

resources

The next sections list resources (books, workshops, audios, videos, Web sites, and organizations) that I believe in and recommend strongly. Each of them will support and empower you on your path of personal growth and discovery. Some of these resources are specifically focused on appreciation and gratitude; some are focused more generally on personal development. I urge you to check out any or all of them.

Books

Many of these books were referenced specifically throughout the book. All these titles are great and will enhance your personal growth:

Ask and It Is Given, by Esther and Jerry Hicks
Awaken the Giant Within, by Anthony Robbins
A Carrot a Day, by Adrian Gostick and Chester Elton
Chicken Soup for the Single Parent's Soul, by Jack Canfield and
    Mark Victor Hansen
Conscious Loving, by Gay and Kathlyn Hendricks
Conversations with God, by Neale Donald Walsh

The Dark Side of the Light Chasers, by Debbie Ford

Don't Sweat the Small Stuff, by Richard Carlson

Emotional Intelligence, by Daniel Goleman

Excuse Me, Your Life Is Waiting, by Lynn Grabhorn

Extreme Success, by Rich Fettke

Forget Perfect, by Lisa Earle McLeod and JoAnn Swan

Forgive for Good, by Fred Luskin

The Four Agreements, by don Miguel Ruiz

Gratitude: A Way of Life, by Louise Hay

The Hidden Messages in Water, by Masaru Emoto

How Full Is Your Bucket? by Donald Clifton and Tom Rath

I Need Your Love—Is That True? by Byron Katie

Inspiration, by Wayne Dyer

Keys to the Kingdom, by Alison Armstrong

Learned Optimism, by Martin Seligman

Love Your Body, by Louise Hay

Make Your Creative Dreams Real, by SARK

Nonviolent Communication, by Marshall Rosenberg

Now, Discover Your Strengths, by Marcus Buckingham and
     Donald Clifton

The Power of Appreciation, by Noelle C. Nelson and Jeannine
     Lemare Calaba

The Power of Positive Thinking, by Norman Vincent Peale

The Psychology of Gratitude, by Robert Emmons and Michael
     McCullough

A Return to Love, by Marianne Williamson

Sacred Journey, by Lazaris

The Seven Habits of Highly Effective People, by Stephen Covey

Simple Abundance, by Sarah Ban Breathnach
Taming Your Gremlin, by Rick Carson
Tuesdays with Morrie, by Mitch Albom
Way of the Peaceful Warrior, by Dan Millman
The Way of the Superior Man, by David Deida
Why Talking Is Not Enough, by Susan Page
Will You Still Love Me If I Don't Win? by Christopher Andersonn
You Can Heal Your Life, by Louise Hay

Workshops

The Abounding River www.withthecurrent.com
The Arete Experience www.aretecenter.com
Celebrating Men, Satisfying Women (for women only)
        www.understandingmen.com
The Landmark Forum www.landmarkforum.com
The New Warrior Training Adventure (for men only)
        www.mkp.org
The Next Step www.challengeday.org
The Shadow Process www.integrativecoaching.com

Other Resources

"Appreciation in Action" (monthly e-mail newsletter)
        www.mike-robbins.com
Appreciative Inquiry (consulting company based on
        appreciation) www.aiconsulting.org
Café Gratitude (inspiring raw food café)
        www.withthecurrent.com
Challenge Day (amazing youth peace organization)
        www.challengeday.org

Go Gratitude (Web site and project focused on gratitude)
    www.gogratitude.com
Nonviolent Communications (incredible conflict
    resolution work) www.cnvc.org
The Peace Alliance (international peace organization)
    www.thepeacealliance.org
The Power of Appreciation (audio program), by Mike Robbins
    www.mike-robbins.com
The Secret (DVD) www.thesecret.tv
What the Bleep Do We Know!? (movie) www.whatthebleep.com
Winning Strategies (boxed set of personal development
    audiotapes and videos) www.mike-robbins.com

about the author

Mike Robbins delivers motivational keynote addresses, personal development workshops, and coaching programs for individuals, groups, and organizations. He works with Fortune 500 companies, government agencies, nonprofits, and individuals from all walks of life. Through his speaking, coaching, and consulting business, Mike empowers people to be successful, create extraordinary relationships, and appreciate themselves and those around them.

Prior to becoming a professional speaker, author, and coach, Mike played baseball at Stanford University and then played professionally with the Kansas City Royals. After his baseball career was cut short by injuries, he worked in advertising sales and business development for two Internet start-up companies.

Mike is a contributing author to *Chicken Soup for the Single Parent's Soul* and the author of the audio program *The Power of Appreciation*.

Mike lives with his wife, Michelle, and their daughter, Samantha, in the San Francisco Bay Area.

For more information on Mike's work and his keynotes, seminars, and other services, feel free to visit www.mike-robbins.com.